New Directions in
Tropical Asian Architecture

Philip Goad
Anoma Pieris

Photography
Patrick Bingham-Hall

Architect Profiles
and Project Descriptions
Philip Goad
Anoma Pieris
Amanda Achmadi

Photography Captions
Philip Goad

Editor
Patrick Bingham-Hall

PERIPLUS

Published by Periplus Editions, with editorial offices at
130 Joo Seng Road #06-01, Singapore 368357.

Editor: Patrick Bingham-Hall
Design: Mark Thacker – Big Cat Design
All photography © Patrick Bingham-Hall 2005
Text © Pesaro Publishing and authors as marked

ISBN 0-7946-0318-1

Distributed by
North America, Latin America & Europe
Tuttle Publishing
364 Innovation Drive
North Clarendon, VT 05759-9436
Tel: (802) 773 8930
Fax: (802) 773 6993
Email: info@tuttlepublishing.com
www.tuttlepublishing.com

Japan
Tuttle Publishing, Yaekari Building, 3F
5-4-12 Osaki, Shinagawa-ku
Tokyo 141-0032
Tel: (03)5437 0171
Fax: (03) 5437 0755
Email: tuttle-sales@gol.com

Asia Pacific
Berkeley Books Pte Ltd
130 Joo Seng Road #06-01/03
Singapore 368357
Tel: (65) 6280 1330
Fax: (65) 6280 6290
Email: inquiries@periplus.com.sg
www.periplus.com

Printed in Singapore

09 08 07 06 05
5 4 3 2 1

New Directions in
Tropical Asian Architecture

Philip Goad

In the next decade, tropical Asia will not just dominate a large portion of the West's production of architecture in its capacity as a service provider[1] but it will also consolidate its position as a centre in its own right. It will become the location for extraordinary central urban expansion and massive infrastructural development, and it will experience unprecedented demand for middle-class suburban housing. At the same time, there will be a need to reconcile extremes of wealth and poverty, to address the alarming gulf between those who are housed well and those who are not, and to broach the challenge of ecological sustainability: not just in a material and technical sense, but in the broader scheme of an everyday amenity and an urbanism that has some measure of longevity. This part of the world will be the location for extreme cultures of congestion in countries where identity is alternately contested, traded, at times resisted, and occasionally where identity simply goes willingly unacknowledged.

The rationale for an examination of new directions in contemporary tropical Asian architecture is not hard to find. First and foremost, it is simply overdue. No previous text has attempted to give an overview of the myriad of design paths open to practitioners in the region.[2] This may have been due to the extremes of practice that deter any succinct overview. In a part of the globe where the practice of design oscillates between First, Second and Third World economies, and their associated politics and ethical limits, making generalised statements is risky, even dangerous. Yet given the exponential growth, wealth and occasional poverty of cities such as Mumbai, Bangkok and Jakarta, located in densely settled countries with massive populations (India over 800 million and Indonesia over 230 million), the region demands attention.

Kuala Lumpur skyline –
August 2004.

1 See P Tombesi, B Dave, and
P Scriver, 'Routine Production
or Symbolic Analysis? India
and the Globalisation of
Architectural Services', *The
Journal of Architecture*, 8:
1, 2003, pp63-94 and P
Tombesi, 'A True South for
Design' The New International
Division of Labour in
Architecture', *Architectural
Research Quarterly*, 5: 2, 2001,
pp171-180.

2 The closest exception to this
statement is the outcome of the
November 1998 symposium
Tropical Encounter organised
by the Institute for Tropical
Architecture in San Jose, Costa
Rica, published as A Tzonis,
L Lefaivre and B Stagno (eds.),
*Tropical architecture: Critical
Regionalism in the Age of
Globalization*, London:
Wiley-Academy, 2001.

3 M Fry and J Drew, *Tropical
architecture in the humid zone*,
London: Batsford, 1956. The
popularity of this text meant
that in 1964 it was updated and
expanded and reissued as
*Tropical architecture: in the dry
and humid zones*, London:
Batsford, c1964.

The location for this selective glimpse is tropical Asia, a slice of geography that straddles the Equator, a region that includes much of the Indian sub-continent, the islands of Sri Lanka and Singapore, the peninsulas of Thailand and Malaysia, and the world's largest archipelago: Indonesia. The observant will quickly point out that there are some countries missing – Burma, Cambodia, Vietnam, Philippines and Laos – but the thesis outlined here is openly admitted to be contingent. It does not attempt to be all-inclusive. This is the second reason for compiling such a book. It represents one step, amongst many possible others, in opening up the region to greater scrutiny, to a greater embrace of its complexity. It provides documentation that will stimulate self-reflexive analysis, rather than analysis that is reliant on Western benchmarks of what is deemed to be 'good', and in this regard the author acknowledges his status as interloper.

In earlier books that looked at strategies for designing contemporary architecture in the region, especially Maxwell Fry and Jane Drew's *Tropical Architecture in the Humid Zone* (1956)[3] and Victor Olgyay and Aladar Olgyay's *Design with Climate: Bioclimatic Approach to Architectural Regionalism* (1963),[4] the common theme was climate, as a determining agent in the inexorable

spread of Modernism as the appropriate functionalist tool for promoting the 'new architecture' in the decade following World War II. There were limits and potentials to these authors' readings of climate and material practices: reinforced concrete, for example, was seen by many as a permanent panacea to the ephemerality of vernacular construction techniques. But one of the results of such an approach was that it liberated local architectures from the mantle of the immediately colonial, especially the bungalow and the imperial overtones of the classicism that had so dominated earlier public buildings. It also wrested these same architectures from the vernacular, and plunged them forthwith into an embrace of a globally accepted hegemony, the reinforced concrete frame. No clear thesis has yet been written on Fry and Drew's legacy, the hybrid educational experiences of local architects and the presence of educators like German émigré/exile Julius Posener in cities such as Kuala Lumpur during the 1950s.[5] But the implications are clear. Modernism in tropical Asia has yet to be fully processed as an idea, as a vehicle for invariably overseas-trained (but locally born) architects proposing afresh, establishing local design cultures at the same time as virtually all of these countries emerged from colonial status – India in 1947, Sri Lanka in 1948, Indonesia in 1949, Malaysia in 1957, and Singapore's ceding from Malaysia in 1965.[6]

The third reason for this book's rationale is that the discourse which has recently arisen from this region has been mired in stereotype. Global tourism has engendered a specific type of publishing response to architecture of this region, and in doing so has come to create myths that are not just inspired by seductive images, but have been the major avenue for many of the best architects of this region to gain international attention. In doing so, local critics and historians have laboured within this specialised, and arguably narrow, market to steer a course of criticism, which, while virtuous, has largely foundered on a singular focus on the 'tropical house' or the 'tropical resort'.[7] Other texts which have emerged from universities and from the pens of committed individuals like William SW Lim, Charles Correa, Tay Kheng Soon and Ken Yeang have argued valiantly for the region's theoretical complexity, but these authors, acting as not just commentators, but also as architects, have yet to receive a corresponding criticism. The flow of discourse has been decidedly one-way.

The time has come to attempt to characterise this moment, to make some claims for broad design themes, but with the qualification that this book will only hint at the complexities inherent to practice in the area of the world that might be described as tropical Asia. There are eleven architects/firms featured in the book, which is another of its acknowledged limits. Additionally, many of the architects featured in this book are relatively young (some in their early forties or younger), and a number are women, indicating changed circumstances in the nature of practising within the region. The majority of the architects have been trained elsewhere and have returned, bringing within them a heightened sense of where they came from and where they are now – the perspective of returning home. This selective focus thus allows scope for further voices

to be added by others. Indeed that is one of the book's major aims.

Six design themes have been suggested for mapping new directions in tropical Asian architecture: reflections on the historic Asian city; reflections on the emerging Asian metropolis; material practices as key determinants to new practice; the need to understand and work beyond Modernism; the need to understand and work beyond the idea of region and the success of the tropical resort; and the potential in tropical Asia, for the idea of a 'minor architecture' to have major consequences, to realise unseen potential and shape new directions.

4 V Olgyay and A Olgyay, *Design with climate: bioclimatic approach to architectural regionalism*, Princeton, N.J., Princeton University Press, 1963. Other writings on climate and architecture at the time included: M Danby, *Grammar of architectural design, with special reference to the tropics*, London: Oxford University Press, 1963; SE Trotter, *Cities in the Sun*, Brisbane: St. Regis-ACI, 1963; and B Singh Saini, *Tropical building research, Territory of Papua and New Guinea: excerpts from a preliminary report*, Port Moresby, 1963

5 Julius Posener (1904-1996) was an influential German art historian who emigrated from Berlin to Palestine in 1935, became a British citizen in 1941, and from 1956 until 1961 spent six years teaching in Kuala Lumpur and became a critical figure in the promotion of modernist architecture in postwar Malaysia. In 1961, he returned to Berlin to write and teach until his death in 1996.

6 The first text to address this phenomenon any detail is M Crinson, *Modern architecture and the end of empire*, Burlington, VT: Ashgate, 2002.

7 In this regard, the prolific output of writers like Robert Powell and Tan Hock Beng has ensured that worldwide attention has been focussed on Southeast Asia's contemporary architecture. See, for example, Robert Powell's *The Asian House: Contemporary Houses of Southeast Asia*, Singapore: Select Publishing, 1993; *The New Asian House*, Singapore: Select Publishing, 2001; *The New Singapore House*, Singapore: Select Publishing, 2001; *The New Thai House*, Singapore: Select Publishing, 2003; *The Tropical Asian House*, London: Thames & Hudson, 1996; and *The Urban Asian House: Living in Tropical Cities*, London: Thames & Hudson, 1998. Tan Hock Beng has authored *Tropical Resorts*, Singapore: Page One Publishing, c1995; *Indonesian accents: architecture, interior design, art*, New York, N.Y.: Visual Reference, 1999 and with W Lim, *Contemporary vernacular: evoking traditions in Asian architecture*, Singapore: Select Books, c1998.

Chowmahalla Palace, Hyderabad, India c.1750. Restoration by Rahul Mehrotra 2002–

Below: Expo MRT Station, Singapore 2002. Architect – Foster and Partners

OLD CITY: REFLECTIONS

In the haste of postwar development, accelerated by the 1960s rise of nationalism and independence, where modern architecture became the byword for progress and change, the historic city in Asia was often the victim of large scale *tabula rasa* functionalist planning. Sometimes this had catastrophic infrastructural implications, such as Kuala Lumpur's half-complete rail and freeway network, or the meticulous over-planning of Singapore, where the historic city was effectively parcelled away and drained of the life that once ran through its streets. The results for Singapore were sanitised touristic environments where any traces of the gritty mix of cultures are now only evident in such locations as Little India or in the ephemerality of the daily wet markets beneath Housing and Development Board (HDB) apartment blocks. Large scale monuments of the colonial era survived, but to a large degree entire residential and commercial districts vanished, when

designations of historic and social significance pinned to a single building could not sustain the retention of general urban fabric. These were the precincts that suffered devastation and disappearance. Indeed, the modern Asian metropolis is largely a story of condoned disappearance.

In spite of this, in many Asian cities in the late 1960s and 1970s, as occurred elsewhere around the world, heritage and conservation efforts realised the retention of some areas of value. Also understood was the value of urban morphology as an aid to an understanding of how to build with the historic city rather than excise it from view. In Sri Lanka, Ronald Lewcock and Barbara Sansoni's efforts over many years in popularising and documenting historic Sri Lankan architecture engendered a consciousness of the importance of memory.[8] Geoffrey Bawa's own house in Colombo (1969), for example, was a skilful amalgamation of four existing houses into one. In Surabaya, the efforts

8 The culmination of this work was R Lewcock, B Sansoni and L Senanayake, *The architecture of an island: the living legacy of Sri Lanka*, Colombo: Barefoot (Pvt.) Ltd, 1998.

9 The Kampung Kebalen Improvement Program, Surabaya, Indonesia, completed in 1981 was the recipient of an honourable mention in the 1984-1986 (third) cycle of the Aga Khan Award for Architecture.

10 KL Lee, *The Singapore house 1819-1942*, Singapore: Times Editions [for] Preservation of Monuments Board, 1988; JSH Lim, 'The Shophouse in Colonial Singapore: Origins and Prototypes', *Asia-Australasia*, Papers from the Annual Conference of the Society of Architectural Historians, Australia and New Zealand, Geelong, 1992; R Powell, *Living legacy: Singapore's architectural heritage renewed*, Singapore: Singapore Heritage Society and Select Books, c1994.

11 S Dwivedi and R Mehrotra, *Bombay: the Cities Within*, Bombay: India Book House, c1995.

12 R Marshall, *Emerging Urbanity: Global Urban Projects in the Asia Pacific Rim*, Spon Press, London, 2003.

13 Another of Singapore's architecturally advanced rail stations is the recent MRT station (2004) at Changi International Airport by US firm, Skidmore Owings & Merrill.

of Professor Johan Silas with the Surabaya Institute of Technology in interpreting the housing form and type of the traditional *kampong* form earned international recognition with an Aga Khan honourable mention in 1984-86.[9] In Singapore, the efforts of Lee Kip Lin, Robert Powell and Jon Lim in documenting the typology of the Chinese shophouse realised a new awareness of the type.[10] Indeed, sensitive refurbishment of shophouses by Kerry Hill, SCDA and WOHA indicate that the limits imposed by heritage protection can and should produce innovation.

It is this understanding of the historic Asian city that informs the work of an architect such as Rahul Mehrotra. For a number of young architects, working through the limits of heritage can reveal new ideas based deep within the psyche of the historic Asian city. It is no surprise that architects of material skill, such as the Italian Carlo Scarpa, the Swede Jan Gezellius, and more recently the Swiss Peter Zumthor, cut their teeth on working with historic buildings: reconstructing, studying, and adding subtly. The intricacies of detail and scale required understanding, and a humble insertion or the grafting of new onto old required skill equal to that of the hero architect. Mehrotra's mode of practice has become singular in the region in terms of his intimate knowledge of his city[11] – Mumbai – and his expert knowledge of the history of Indian architecture informs his new work. It is this approach to practice that each Asian city needs and should be able to sustain. For it is through practice such as this that the echo of memory is possible. So much discussion of the Asian city today focuses on the new and the futuristic, as if the past has no future, but in the historic Asian city there are new discoveries to be made that lie outside the realm of pure notions of heritage. For the designer, there are questions of grain size, morphology, movement patterns, scale and density which may suggest the vibrancy of urban life sometimes missing from the vitally new. This is the time for genuine design-based reflection, analysis and speculation on the old cities of Asia – on Melaka, on Chennai, on Hanoi, on Kandy, on Chiang Mai. For here, there will be found new spirits lurking within the old which will give real difference to the new cities of Asia.

NEW CITY: REFLECTIONS

In the growth of the contemporary metropolis, the 21st century will belong to the Asia Pacific region. Cities such as Singapore, Jakarta, Bangkok, Mumbai and Shanghai will, as Richard Marshall convincingly argues,

'globally position' themselves.[12] Characteristics of this positioning will be: accelerated urban redevelopment; the commissioning of signature architects (at times much to the justified dismay of local professionals); the introduction of advanced infrastructure such as Bangkok's new Metro (1999-2004) and Singapore's glistening new Expo MRT station (2002) designed by Foster Associates[13]; the adoption of hyper-mall shopping experiences such as Suria KLCC in Kuala Lumpur; and a highlighting of the gap between a controlling elite and a service-providing class, either from within the city or more commonly from without; such migrant workers commuting from distant but affordable satellite centres. Such theorists as Gülsüm Nalbantoglu and Wong Chong Thai, Gayatryi Chakravorty Spivak, Brenda Yeoh, Ackbar Abbas, Stephen Cairns and others[14] have edited works on, or written persuasively of the potential social and political alienation that this urban phenomenon creates and has created. But such theoretical critiques while valuable are not enough. There are calls to action that require serious adoption and testing at a physical level: at the level of design.

Important design speculations on the tropical city by eminent local architects such as Ken Yeang, William SW Lim, Sumet Jumsai and Tay Kheng Soon need not just testing but ongoing documentation and analysis.[15] Their work needs consolidation by a younger generation prepared to critique their eloquent elders and move beyond them. Equally critical is the responsibility of local schools of architecture to promote these practitioners as a way of instilling a culture of urban research, to reflect on the phenomenon that is the new tropical city. One critical step could be implementation by government authorities and private development interests. A case in point is the initiative of Singapore's Urban Redevelopment Authority's Duxton Plain Public Housing competition (2002), a project which in its scope and ambition should rank, as an historical moment, with Berlin's IBA Housing project (1984), as a critical document of the time on housing and urbanism. On a site of 2.51 hectares, competitors were asked to place 1800 dwelling units in buildings that were to be no more than 50 storeys in height. The aim was high-density high rise urban living, a sort of utopic vision predictive of a future Singapore of 5.5 million people.[16] Another example is the recent creation of Biopolis (2002-2004), a 'science hub' occupying 18.5 hectares of land at the 'one-north' precinct in Singapore, and currently comprising seven interconnected buildings. The 2001 master plan was described by its architect London-based Zaha Hadid as an 'undulating urban

14 GB Nalbantoglu and CT Wong (eds.), *Postcolonial Space(s)*, New York: Princeton Architectural Press, c1997; GC Spivak, *The post-colonial critic: interviews, strategies, dialogues*, New York: Routledge, c1990; M Gandelsonas, A Abbas, and MC Boyer, *Shanghai reflections: architecture, urbanism and the search for an alternative modernity*, Princeton, New Jersey: Princeton University School of Architecture, 2002; S Cairns (ed.), *Drifting: architecture and migrancy*, New York: Routledge, 2004; BSA Yeoh, *Contesting space : power relations and the urban built environment in colonial Singapore*, Kuala Lumpur; New York: Oxford University Press, 1996; RBH Goh, Brenda SA Yeoh (eds.), *Theorizing the Southeast Asian City as text: urban landscapes, cultural documents, and interpretative experiences*, Singapore: World Scientific Pub., 2003.

15 WSW Lim, *Asian new urbanism and other papers*, Singapore: Select Books, c1998; WSW Lim (ed.), *Postmodern Singapore*, Singapore: Select Publishers, 2002; WSW Lim, *Alternative (post)modernity: an Asian perspective*, Singapore: Select Publishers, 2003; KS Tay, *Mega-cities in the tropics: towards an architectural agenda for the future*, Singapore: Institute of Southeast Asian Studies, 1989; KS Tay & Arkitek Tenggara / R Powell, *Line edge & shade: the search for a design language in tropical Asia*, Singapore: Page One Publishing, 1997; J Sumet, *Naga: cultural origins in Siam and the West Pacific*, Oxford University Press, Singapore, 1988; K Yeang (ed.), *Bioclimatic skyscrapers*, London : Artemis, 1994; K Yeang, *The skyscraper bioclimatically considered: a design primer*, London: Academy Editions, 1996; K Yeang, *The green skyscraper: the basis for designing sustainable intensive buildings*, Munich : Prestel, c1999; K Yeang, *Reinventing the skyscraper: a vertical theory of urban design*, Chichester : Wiley-Academy, 2002; K Yeang, *Designing for survival: architecture and ecological design*, New York; Chichester: Wiley, 2004.

16 As outlined in the URA's 2001 Concept Plan for Singapore. The brief and description of competition entries can be found in *Duxton Plain Public Housing: International Architectural Design Competition*, Urban Redevelopment Authority, Singapore, 2002.

Rujinarong, Pornchai Boonsom and Duangrit Bunnag in Thailand, the clientele has moved beyond regional nostalgia. For them, the everyday of the new Asian city is air-conditioned, efficient, internalised and deliberately placeless. The architectural language of their new Asian city is globally familiar. The lack of nostalgia, the complete embrace of the hermetic globally-aware workplace and consumer environment means that notions of tropicality are set aside. The challenge, then, is self-conscious realisation of that state, and the decision to embrace that heightened state and theorise and design with it. Or, for a younger generation of architects and urbanists, to determine a more cunning interpretation, similar to that which Japanese architects realised in the 1960s, that their cities were deep, that the palimpsest of culture, climate and place might not impede global positioning but in fact differentiate such a position, and make it unique.

MATERIAL PRACTICE: REFLECTIONS

India is not Singapore, nor is it Malaysia, and Sri Lanka is not Indonesia, nor is it Thailand. Each place is different and this means that architecture can be, and often is, different across the region. Any major difference is due primarily to local material and construction practices. Understanding material practices as an aid to location and identity is a key factor in any appreciation of contemporary tropical Asian architecture. It is what gave, and still does give, the work of many Asian architects of the region their obvious distinction. Vernacular craft traditions can be found and deployed. Architects such as Jimmy Lim, Ernesto Bedmar, Bobby Mañosa and Geoffrey Bawa in their residential and hotel designs, and Soejano & Rachman with the Soekarno-Hatta International Airport in Jakarta (1985), have capitalised on this, employing traditional stone and timber details and construction techniques. It is these distinctive material practices of a perceived Asian vernacular (as well as colonial practices) that have determined the popularity of the tropical resort. This is an obvious platitude. But the reality is such that in a country such as Sri Lanka, the work of Anura Ratnavibushana, and in Indonesia, the work of Eko Prawoto, is determined by local craft capabilities, and the work of Adi Purnomo, Andra Matin and Ahmad Djuhara in Jakarta is further determined by the need to investigate low-cost alternatives. It is these material practices, consciously embraced, which root much of the work in the now much-cited and still relevant position of a critical regionalism.[17]

carpet', and its ambitions were a freer and more fluid attempt at masterplanning in Singapore, and with an enticing spatial proximity between knife-edged profiled buildings and flyover bridge connections. In both these initiatives, the test will be whether the hopeful aspirations of the competition brief and the master plan are realised not just formally but also at the level of complex patterns of everyday urban life. Most positively however – experiment, even risk, has been embraced.

Ambitious global positioning has already realised an economically mobile and culturally independent wealthy middle class, demanding (in home and investment opportunity) two specific dwelling outcomes: luxury highrise apartments and detached villas. A critical dilemma is thus raised for architects practising in such an environment. For architects such as WOHA, W Architects and SCDA in Singapore, and Tinakorn

By contrast, in cities such as Bangkok, Kuala Lumpur and Singapore, the material practices are almost all dictated by Western speculative building practice and an import market that draws from the rich stone quarries of Java and migrant labour from India and Bangladesh. There is danger, therefore, in attempting to generalise across the region. But it can be said that overall, the material practices of tropical Asia, apart from the house and hotel, have been dominated by the reinforced concrete frame as a constant template for form since the 1940s. And as such, it has been explored for its formal and symbolic capabilities. In the hands of Le Corbusier, reinforced concrete became the sculptural plasticine for Punjab's expression of monumental statehood. It defined the civic language of Chandigarh, as well as other cities like Ahmedabad. In Malaysian architect Hijjas Kasturi's Luth Building (1986) and Menara Maybank Building (1982-87), both in Kuala Lumpur, reinforced concrete was the expressive medium for his "struggle to provide a recognizable, ethnic-based cultural symbolism."[18]

The architects in this book fall into both areas of practice. Architects such as Cheong Yew Kuan, Kanika Ratanapridakul, Rahul Mehrotra, Eko Prawoto and Kevin Low adopt a restrained material practice, determining a quiet resistance to the hegemony of glass and lightweight panels covering the reinforced concrete frame and to the tendency to over-embellish. By contrast, the Singapore-based architects Kerry Hill, WOHA, SCDA and W Architects embrace the entire palette of available material and construction practices. WOHA's St Mary of the Angels in Singapore (2003) is exemplary in its richness of materials, but also in the dexterity with which those materials have been deployed. The result is a reflection not just of the wealth of the parish and the clientele, but also of the compositional range of the architects. Interestingly, across all the work, the predominance of stone, concrete and rendered surfaces means that much of this recent tropical architecture is concerned with mass, rather than perpetuating preconceptions of Asian architecture as lightweight, timber and relatively ephemeral. The truth is quite the reverse. In reality, the idea of a lightweight architecture is to be found in the work of the dry construction trades, in the predominantly Western cladding practices of glass, steel, and the aluminium window frame. In all of these choices open to the architect, difference is determined by the hand-based (hence largely anachronistic) act of building or making, but an act that nevertheless, if consciously understood, reveals potential for new directions in architectural design.

BEYOND MODERNISM

In the 1960s and early 1970s, the language of orthodox Modernism became the language of national independence and a symbol of progress. Architects, born in the region but invariably trained in the 1950s and 1960s in Great Britain (often attending the Architectural Association's course on tropical architecture), Australia and the United States, or having worked with one or more of the 'masters' of Modern architecture (such as Le Corbusier at Chandigarh) began to deploy the material practices and functionalist planning of Modernism. They practised either on their own or within transformed inherited colonial practices such as Booty, Edwards & Partners in Malaysia (later to become BEP) and new group practices like the Malayan Architects Co-Partnership,[19] which later became the Singapore-based Design Partnership[20] in emulation of Walter Gropius's team-driven ideal of modern practice, TAC (The Architects Collaborative) and the London-based Architects Co-Partnership. The use of reinforced concrete, the *brise soleil*, broad oversailing eaves and parasol roofs to monumental pavilions appeared to indicate that orthodox Modernism had been acclimatised by the tropics, and that the task of emulation had been successfully translated to the East.

But the reality is that the work of architects such as Balkrishna Doshi, Charles Correa, Kingston Loo, Minette da Silva, Valentine Gunasekara and the various team practices represent more complex readings of Modernism. These are readings transformed by local insertions, not just of planning techniques and climatic control, but also with decorative schema, entire parti and formal ideas that derive directly from the region. Thus, as Jiat-Hwee Chang has argued, using the theories of Homi Bhabha, such modernisms of the region are better understood as hybrid modernities, instances where exchange, negotiation, translation and reinterpretation are more instructive terms than emulation or subservience to canonical models.[21]

Similar complex readings of Modernism thus need to be understood when appreciating the work of architects such as Andra Matin in Jakarta, Duangrit Bunnag in Bangkok, and Hiranti Welandawe in Colombo. The aims no longer embody the reforming zeal of the 1950s, nor the ambitious social/urban programmes of Design Partnership in the 1970s, but in many respects, signal a return to first principles, to beginning again. This next generation has moved beyond the attractive formal signs of a so-called regional architecture, to a re-thinking of the fundamental issues of space, material

Opposite Louvrebox House
Gita Bayu, Malaysia 2004
Architect – Kevin Low

17 See K Frampton, "Towards a Critical Regionalism: Six points of an architecture of resistance", in H Foster (ed.), *The Anti-aesthetic: essays on postmodern culture*, Port Townsend, Washington: Bay Press, 1983, pp16-30.

18 WSW Lim, 'Nowhere to Somewhere and Beyond', in K Frampton, WSW Lim and J Taylor (eds.), *World Architecture 1900-2000: A Critical Mosaic*, vol.10 (Southeast Asia and Oceania), China Architecture & Building Press, SpringerWien, New York, 1999, pxxiv, 108-109.

19 The Malayan Architects Co-Partnership was headed by three British trained architects, Lim Chong Keat, Chen Voon Fee and William SW Lim.

20 Design Partnership, based in Singapore, was headed by William SW Lim, Goh Siew-Chuan and Tay Kheng Soon.

21 JH Chang, 'Hybrid modernities and tropical architecture in Southeast Asia', *DOCOMOMO*, 29, September 2003, pp76-81.

22 I de Solà-Morales, "Architecture and Existentialism", *Differences: Topographies of Contemporary Architecture*, Cambridge, Mass.: MIT Press, 1995, pp41-55.

23 For example: HB Tan, *Tropical resorts,* Singapore: Page One Pub., c1995; M Wijaya, *Tropical garden design,* London: Thames & Hudson, 1999; P Goad, P Bingham-Hall, *Architecture Bali: Architectures of Welcome,* Periplus, 2000, as well as the many books on contemporary architecture by R Powell. See footnote 7.

24 See L Mumford, "The Skyline", *The New Yorker,* 11 October 1947, pp94-96, 99; P Belluschi, "The Meaning of Regionalism in Architecture", *Architectural Record,* December 1955, pp131-139; and P Rudolph, "Regionalism in Architecture", *Perspecta,* 4, 1957, pp12-19.

Amandari, Ubud, Bali 1987–88. Architect – Peter Muller

practice, tropicality, sustainability, urbanity and place – in essence a return to Ignasi de Sola Morales's 'ground zero' for architecture, a sort of phenomenological and existential base for the production of architecture that existed after World War II.[22]

In the digital age, amid cultures totally at ease with the comfortable placelessness of hermetic environments, such claims for a revisiting of Modernism might seem far-fetched, even sentimental. But the architects of the region understand this. They are not immune to the design tactics embedded within the digital world, nor are they immune to the critique of global capital. Nor are they ignorant of the utopic visions of the preceding generation. But the Modernism they follow must be critical. It will only have effect if it enters the local discourse through media, exposure and dissemination, and only if its efforts touch the everyday as well as the exceptional.

BEYOND REGION AND RESORT

A peculiar aspect of tropical Asian architecture has been the spectre of success following the interpretation of the vernacular through exclusive resort architecture, and its subsequent popularisation through dozens of lavishly illustrated monographs.[23] At the same time that architectural theorists were defining notions of a critical regionalism in the 1980s, in effect updating regionalist ideas which had resurfaced in the late 1940s and 1950s through the writings of Lewis Mumford, Paul Rudolph

and Pietro Belluschi[24], the hotels of Peter Muller and Palmer & Turner in Bali, Ed Tuttle in Thailand and Indonesia, and Geoffrey Bawa in Sri Lanka (amongst a score of others), were receiving deserved international attention.[25] All were highly accomplished, beautifully crafted, and exceptional exercises in the creation of place, ambience, and spatial sequence. Bawa's work in particular, in its translation of Dutch and British colonial typologies, in his eclectic furniture choice and in his ability to re-use existing buildings and building elements struck a chord internationally as an authentic reaction, not just to the rationalist excesses of postwar Functionalism, but also to the facile frippery of much Post Modernist architecture.[26] Critical also to their success was the sympathetic treatment of landscape as an intrinsic element of the entire hotel experience.[27] Bawa's Triton Hotel at Ahungalla, Sri Lanka (1981) and Muller's Amandari, Ubud, Bali (1987-88) were brilliant expositions in building with the landscape. These masterworks spawned a progeny of kitsch reproductions and cast grave doubt over the strategy of creatively reinterpreting traditional architectural forms. Yet the construction and craft industry that surrounds these hotels and their associated service industries has been seen by some commentators such as Michel Picard, particularly with respect to Bali, to have positive outcomes, of sustaining local cultures of economic and artistic production when they were at the risk of being lost.[28]

A key figure in the success of tropical resort architecture has been Kerry Hill, whose initial work for Palmer & Turner at the Bali Hyatt (1972-73) was followed by hotels such as the Aga Khan Award-winning Datai, Langkawi, Malaysia (1993), Balina Serai, Manggis, Bali (1994) and Amanusa, Nusa Dua, Bali (1988-92). The work of his practice has developed further, with a new series of hotels where the vernacular has been shelved in favour of a mature design approach, which suggests new directions for resort architecture. Hill's compositional tactics and choice of forms in hotel and house designs have transcended obvious notions of region, and what the tropical resort and tropical house might be. With his recent hotels in Kolkata, Cairo and Taiwan, and in a private house at Sunshine Beach, Australia, Hill shows a level of abstraction, a rigour in formal grouping and a sophistication of detail that suggests mastery over his art.

Kerry Hill has also mentored an entirely new generation of young architects. Coming out of his Singapore office and successfully setting up practice have been Richard Hassell and Wong Mun Summ of WOHA, and Cheong

Sonar Bangla Hotel, Kolkata,
India 2003.
Architect – Kerry Hill

25 Hotels like Palmer &
Turner's Bali Hyatt, Sanur,
Bali, 1972-74; Bawa's Bentota
Beach Hotel, Bentota, 1969;
Club Villa, Bentota, 1979;
Triton Ahungulla, 1981; Tuttle's
Amanpuri, Phuket, Thailand,
1988; Amankila, Manggis,
Bali, 1993 and Amanjiwo,
Borobodur, 1997; and Peter
Muller's Hotel Oberoi,
Seminyak, 1972-74, 78-99;
Amandari, Ubud, Bali, 1987-88;
and Lombok Oberoi, Medana
Beach, Lombok, 1992-96.

26 Geoffrey Bawa has been
the subject of two important
monographs, namely BB Taylor,
Geoffrey Bawa, Singapore:
Concept Media, 1986 and D
Robson, *Geoffrey Bawa: the
complete works*, New York,
N.Y.: Thames & Hudson, 2002.

27 In Bali, the most significant
figure in the promotion of
sophisticated landscape design
in relation to resort architecture
has been Australia-born Michael
White who changed his name
to Made Wijaya once he made
Bali his permanent home.

28 M Picard and RE Wood
(eds.), *Tourism, ethnicity, and
the state in Asian and Pacific
societies*, Honolulu, Hawaii :
University of Hawai'i Press,
c1997.

29 The concept of lineage
and legacy of the OMA office
is discussed in detail in B
Colenbrander, *reference oma:
the sublime start of an
architectural generation*, NaI
Publishers, Rotterdam, 1995.
For example, important
contemporary practitioners who
have worked for OMA include:
Willem Jan Neuteings; Winy
Maas and Jacob van Rijs, both
of mvrdv; Matthias Sauerbruch
and Louisa Hutton; and Mike
Guyer of the Swiss firm, Gigon
& Guyer.

30 J Bloomer, "Minor
Architectural Possibilities",
in J Whiteman, J Kipnis &
R Burdett, *Strategies in
Architectural Thinking*,
Cambridge, Mass.: MIT
Press, 1992.

Yew Kuan. As with the OMA office in Rotterdam, which gave rise to a new generation of practitioners in Europe[29], so Hill's office has been a laboratory for working in the tropics, albeit with different outcomes and aims. For example, Cheong Yew Kuan, after working in Hill's office, gained his first works through a hotel commission, designing the five detached residences for the Begawan Giri resort near Ubud. This experience, together with his Hardy House, Sayan, Bali (1997), was a virtual saturation in the techniques and practices of traditional Balinese architecture, in applying *alang-alang* (palm thatch) to the archetypal forms of the *bale*. The Begawan Giri project led to further commissions, but with all these Kuan has gradually and deliberately attempted to leave behind references to an idealised vernacular.

The significant observation is that as a design theme, the resort has been instrumental in the retrieval of fundamental spatial procedures: arrival, sequence, reception, theatre, enclosure and release into the landscape. Importantly practitioners like Kerry Hill

and Cheong Yew Kuan have now moved beyond obvious regionalist and resort munificence to more enduring, as well as experimental, architectural agendas. The liberation, even revelation, of the resort experience has been the recovery of an attitude to space and form that is intrinsic to the region: an attitude which can be applied without the baggage of semiotics or obeisance to a picturesque vernacular.

BEYOND MINOR ARCHITECTURE

Architectural influence is not always dependent on projects of great magnitude. Indeed theorists like Jennifer Bloomer would argue it is with projects, written or built, which occur within the margins, at the edges, and in the interstices of mainstream practice that the opportunities for influence and change might occur.[30] Thus in tropical Asia, projects such as the material experimentalism of the architects of Auroville and Laurie Baker's participatory practice in India, or CJ Anjalendran's SOS Children's Village project in

Rental House for City's Commuters, Bintaro, Jakarta, Indonesia 2002–3. Architect – Andra Matin Architect

Opposite House in Cipete Jakarta, Indonesia 2002 Architect – Andra Matin Architect

experiments. The house becomes a laboratory rather than a trophy. The same can also be said of Kanika Ratanapridakul's work in Thailand, which develops significant themes through a small number of house commissions. Her own family house in Bangkok came to be recognised, not through any intent of her own, as symbolising possibilities for the new contemporary Thai house.[34] Additionally, Ratanapridakul believes that through dedicated teaching at the academy, there is considerable investment in experiment, not necessarily through built projects, but instead through ensuring that the responsibility of critique will be instilled in the next generation of architects who will practice in the region. Such efforts in minor architectures, when collected together, indicate a level of commitment deeply embedded within the realities of investigating a long term future for a vital architecture culture in the region.

Piliyandala, Sri Lanka (1982-86), offer insight into what might continue to be an ethical practice in the region.[31] Such projects invariably emerge from small practices. At other times, it might be an influential idea emerges from within a text, such as Sumet Jumsai's thesis on water and architecture in Thailand.[32] To date, the greater part of discourse on architecture within tropical Asia has been related to the larger questions of national identity and the rise of the global metropolis in Asia – the big questions. Minor architecture has thus understandably been invisible, relative to the built projects and speculations that inspire global awe or appear to satisfy a national priority. Minor architectures are often less photogenic, and therefore less marketable as ideas. Thus for architects who work quietly for a middle class in the suburbs, or for non-profit government organizations, or for those who also teach within universities, their practices establish influence by stealth and modest example.

For example, Andra Matin's temporary rental houses for low-income workers in Bintaro (2002-03) on the outskirts of Jakarta, are small in scale. The tiny box form of a four room unit with shared laundry, kitchen and toilet sits diminutively beneath a metal framed orthogonal parasol that supports roll-down bamboo blinds. Yet, as Amanda Achmadi observes, such units imply larger questions about the scale of the contemporary Asian metropolis, the vast distances required for commuting, and the circumstances for accommodating low-paid workers.[33] Likewise, Malaysian architect Kevin Low's interests in the idea of the 'small project' and the unfinished aspect of what modern architecture might entail, lead to profound

NEW DIRECTIONS

The question remains as to how architecture might take part in the transformation of a region by the apparently unstoppable forces of globalisation. For those architects interested in the resultant quality of the built and urban environment, the task lies in providing and maintaining a high quality in urban and architectural amenity for a greater community beyond those that can afford it. The work illustrated in this book does not act as the work of 'urban guerillas', but rather as that of 'urban jewellers', complicit in the process of patronage, but alternately polemical and resistant in their art. Each project sets benchmarks by example, by testing spatial, material and compositional orthodoxies so that effect might be had by stealth, rather than by the corporate branding of the *grand projét*.

The works shown in this book are not the feted 'global urban projects' that have brought competitive notoriety to their cities and assisted in the 'global positioning' of their city and, by corollary, their nation. Instead, all of these projects are relatively small. Yet their implications are broad. They suggest ways of participating within the growth of the tropical Asian city, but from a position of grounded practice, intelligent to the forces which create the environment around them and mindful of the body politic of their region. Such ways of practice might offer clues for proceeding with architecture elsewhere in the world. In many ways, they are insulated from the pressures (even the responsibilities) of the global project, and that is their strength. Their architecture reveals that influence should, and does, lie in content and intention.

31 For information on CJ Anjalendran's work for the SOS Children's Village and the Hermann Gmeiner School there, see *MIMAR*, 20, 1986.

32 J Sumet, *Naga: cultural origins in Siam and the West Pacific*, Singapore; New York: Oxford University Press, 1988.

33 A Achmadi, "Indonesia: The Emergence of a new architectural consciousness of the urban middle class", in G London (ed.), *Houses for the 21st Century*, Periplus, Singapore 2003, pp28-35.

34 Interview with Kanika Ratanapridakul, June 2004.

The Search for Tropical Identities:
A Critical History

Anoma Pieris

For South and Southeast Asia, the 20th Century was a period of prolonged cultural crisis brought on by the pressures of colonial rule, nascent nationalisms, modern expectations and the pressures of economic globalization. At the centre of this crisis was the need to construct a sense of identity that could accommodate contradictory readings of tradition and modernity, and reinforce the sense of geographic belonging engendered by independence.

Theorized in terms of postcolonial anxieties, these struggles for self-definition have carved out an ideological terrain along which modern nations and their subjects have had to travel. The paths are uneven, beset by a "million mutinies"[1] against the secular state from religious, ethnic and political minorities; modified by the demands of multinational investors and global watch dogs; and driven by cosmopolitan aspirations and desires. Cumulatively these struggles form the cultural landscape of the 20th Century and the emerging history of the 21st Century. Both tradition and modernity were filtered through a particular climatic trope to produce what can been described as Tropical Asian Architecture.

TROPICAL HISTORIES

Tropical Asia took on its identity through a colonial process, extractive and often violent, and which, during the 19th Century, represented the region as a landscape of unpredictable dangers and a feminized object of desire. Its advantage to European imperial interests was in its fertility for industrial agriculture, with the possibility of generating a new crop with every rainy season. But the fertility of this terrain bred varied life forms, benign as well as deadly, which to the colonial mind invited disease, torpor and degeneration. The tropics embodied the chaotic diversity that was cast outside the grid of European rationalism. Colonial literature of the 19th Century used this definition to encircle the Asian colonies described by John Cameron as "Our tropical possessions in Malayan India"[2], thus drawing Britain's Southeast Asian colonies onto the larger map of the Indian subcontinent. As observed by Anthony Reid, Southeast Asia seemed to defy all

generalizations and presented a bewildering variety of languages, cultures and religions, but an adaptation to a common physical environment and a high degree of commercial intercourse gave the region its common character.[3] For colonial architects, the tropical climate produced a distinctive model of colonial life, one associated with bungalows, verandah living and a picturesque setting, which located the building traditions of the colonized outside the predominantly Western tradition of architectural production.

At the 2004 International Conference on Tropical Architecture, Alexander Tzonis called on this climatic imaginary to illustrate what he saw as the contrast between tropical and temperate architectures.[4] In Tzonis's interpretation the temperate climate was captured in the image of a mountain viewed from across a plain, as an object in a landscape. The tropical climate was its antithesis: an image framing the biodiversity of a rain forest, which suggested a more subjective and contextual experience. The opposition of form and context raised by Tzonis was reminiscent of Modernism's ideological separation from the fine grained and historically layered urban environments of Europe. Whereas the harsher climate of northern Europe had provoked such defensive explorations of containment, objectification was alien to the tropics where cross-ventilation, the modulation of light and the preference for materials with low embodied heat suggested a more interactive approach to the external environment. The lesson to be learned from tropical examples was one of managing diversity under consistently hot and humid conditions.

Our perceptions of the tropics, whether from within them or without, seek out this particular heterogeneity most familiar in Orientalist imagery: the bright colours, dappled light and minutiae of biological diversity in a physical equivalent of Paradise. The strength of this idiom is in its blurring of boundaries and with the fluid movement from outside to inside, which allows the man-made landscape to amplify nature. The tropical landscape achieved a dissolution of form by eroding the formal boundaries set up by climatically defensive environments. During the 19th Century it fed off and reciprocally fuelled the Picturesque, resulting in the carefully controlled artlessness of the English garden. While Europe bestowed its colonies with a rational neo-classical template of formal objects (institutional monoliths, self-contained bungalows, city grids and public monuments), the tropical response was closer to the Gothic – a creative individuality that infiltrated the colonial order, creating its own inimical counter-culture.

1 VS Naipaul, *India: a million mutinies now*, London: Heinemann, 1990.

2 J Cameron, *Our tropical possessions in Malayan India*, London: Smith, Elder, 1865.

3 A Reid, *Southeast Asia in the age of commerce, 1450-1680*, New Haven: Yale University Press, 1993, pp4-5.

4 A Tzonis, " Sustainable Social Quality, Rethinking Design Methodology", *iNTA Conference*, National University of Singapore, 26 February 2004.

5 S Chattopadhyay, "A Critical History of Architecture in a Post-Colonial World: A View from Indian History," *Architectronic*, 6:1: http://architronic.saed.kent.edu/v6n1/v6n1.05a.html, p1.

6 K Marx, F Engels, "On Colonialism", *Marx and Engels Collected Works*, Vol.12, Moscow: Progress Publishers, 1853 –54.

7 HK Bhaba, *The location of culture*, London; New York: Routledge, 1994, p35.

8 T Metcalf, *An Imperial Vision: Indian Architecture and Britain's Raj*, Berkeley: University of California Press, 1989, pp211-239.

9 CK Lai, Unpublished paper, 'Tropical Tropes: The architectural politics of building in hot and humid climates', presented at '(Un)bounding Tradition: The tensions of borders and regions', 8th IASTE International Conference, Hong Kong, 12-15 December 2002.

10 Ibid.

11 A Kusno, *Beyond the postcolonial: architecture urban cultures and political space in Indonesia*, London: Routledge, 2000.

12 HG Ross, "Building Cambodia" New Khmer Architecture 1953-1970 –Elements of Tradition Transcended", paper at the *MAAN 2003 Conference*, 29 August 2003.

13 H Fernandez, in Jon Lim (ed.), *Transforming traditions: architecture in the ASEAN countries: Brunei, Malaysia, Indonesia, Philippines, Singapore, Thailand*, Singapore, ASEAN Committee on Culture and Information (COCI), 2001, p147.

14 EH Endut, in Jon Lim (ed.), p103.

15 T Winichakul, *Siam mapped: a history of the geo-body of a nation*, Honolulu: University of Hawaii Press, 1994.

16 V Horayangkura, in J Lim (ed.), 2001, pp223-263.

17 Ibid, p247.

Thus the fragmented episodic nature of the tropical experience located itself at the periphery of architectural discourse, in the so-called "un-self-conscious" realm of vernacular expression. The 'vernacular' was interpreted at two levels: as historic monuments salvaged through colonial archaeological projects; and the 'primitive' bazaar or village architecture of the indigenous populations.[5] While the former were dismissed as products of a once glorious and since extinct civilization, the latter was regarded as the timeless production of a static internal economy, typical of pre-modern agrarian societies. Underlying this categorization was Karl Marx's critique of Asia as the world of feudal despots in what he described as 'hydraulic civilizations'.[6] The architectural counterpoint of these pre-modern architectural traditions was the innovative and creative architecture of European historical styles. Thus the marginalization of the vernacular tradition exposed the prevailing architectural hierarchy, where historicism produced a chronological record of the politically and culturally powerful symbols of Western civilization. Thus the tropical vernacular typically entered the European gaze as part of the Orientalist fare of colonial exhibitions. Its marginalization as an invalid self-expression for a contemporary society reiterated the theft of South and South East identity which had followed colonization.

AN ARCHITECTURE OF IDENTITY

By the early years of the 20th Century, the colonial government in India began to make concessions to local identities by incorporating Indianised forms and motifs in civic architecture. As observed by Homi Bhaba, it adopted "a strategy of representing authority in terms of the artifice of the archaic".[7] In this instance, two forms were combined: the religious architectures (Hindu, Islamic and Buddhist) of Asia with the classical architecture of Europe. Executed by architects of the Public Works Department, and supported by a revival of Arts and Crafts movements both in Britain and in its colonies, these styles had already been tested in palaces for princely rulers and colonial museums. The plan for New Delhi and the Viceroy's Residence (1912-1931), designed by Edwin Lutyens, was the apex of an effort to monumentalize British rule by an architectural hybrid. This would set the stage for a particular strain of cultural ambivalence, which drew liberally from both Eastern and Western sources. As argued by Thomas Metcalf, these styles traveled back to the Western metropolis as architectural ornaments and fabric designs, which placed the subcontinent as the

nexus of British Imperial power.[8] When India gained its independence from Britain in 1947, British architects prescribed these Indic styles as the architectural expression most suited for the civic institutions of a newly independent nation. By then they had also been transposed onto two other early modern architectural styles of the 1920s, De Stijl and Art Deco, which were more adaptable to the apartment blocks, hospitals, cinemas and educational buildings essential for a post-independence society.

Faced with a choice of modern and traditional expressions the initial postcolonial impulse was to embrace European Modernism for national monuments. The nation's right to self-determination needed to be mapped out on a brand new architectural template, one that could erase all past colonial associations. The universal values of the International Style were brought into Asia in the 1950s on the invitation of Indian president Jawarahal Lal Nehru, who asked Le Corbusier to design Chandigharh, a new state capital for Punjab. During this period several European architects, including Maxwell Fry, Jane Drew, Charles and Ray Eames, Edward Durrell Stone, Joseph Stein and Laurie Baker, arrived in India to experiment with new forms of Modernism. As discussed by Lai Chee Kien in his interrogation of the politics behind the tropical 'trope', the colonial discourse re-emerged as a series of conferences held in Europe throughout the 1950s, focusing on the technical, material and climatic conditions of former colonies and their imperatives for development.[9] Following a conference in London in 1953, the Architectural Association in London commenced its diploma in tropical architecture under Maxwell Fry in 1954, and from 1957 onwards under Otto Koenigsberger. Seven years later in 1962, the University of Melbourne began a postgraduate course in tropical architecture.[10] Due to these programmes, aspiring Asian architects from developing countries found an opportunity to be trained in First World economies, in a specific style of Modernism adapted to tropical climates.

During the next decade, Modernism developed as two predominant strains: Expressionist, following the Brazilian School; and New Brutalism, following primarily the work of Paul Rudolph and the architecture of Boston City Hall. In India, Balkrishna Doshi of Team X emerged as the foremost Modernist while in neighbouring Ceylon, this title fell to Valentine Gunasekara. Their architecture defined spaces for new forms of community through expressive forms and innovative engineering. In Indonesia, architect/president Sukarno's guided democracy was symbolized by a phalanx of Modernist buildings including a national monument, the Hotel Indonesia, the Independence Mosque, the Asian Games Complex and the Jakarta Bypass, all of which signified the nation's developmental ambitions.[11] In Cambodia, a New Khmer style combining Angkor sculptural effects with New Brutalism was created by architect Van Molyvann,[12] and in the Philippines, Leandro V Locsin led a new generation of architects to design experimental multistorey office buildings for Makati, a planned urban development.[13] From among these newly independent Asian nations, it was Malaysia that provided the most daring example of a Modernist tower block for its first parliament.[14] Designed by JKR (Jabatan Kerja Raya) and Ivor Shipley in 1963, both the structure and fenestration on this building resembled an Islamic mosaic when viewed from afar.

In comparison with its postcolonial neighbours, Thailand remains an anomaly, a nation that was historically mapped by boundaries established by adjacent colonial states. During the 19th Century, it was forced to resist this same colonial fate through expedient self-colonization.[15] Thailand's eager embrace of European habits combined with royalist loyalties resulted in a see-saw of architectural styles that swung back and forth between Neo-Traditional (early 20th century), Applied Thai (post World War I-1957) and a "golden period" when Western styles were often assimilated directly (1958-1972).[16] Krisda Arunvongse and Jain Kontanarak are among those in the first generation of Thai architects whose signature style was the design of building façades in geometric patterns. The most influential Modernist is Sumet Jumsai, whose design approach ranges from Techno-Aesthetic to Post-Modernism.

The Modernism of the 1950s to the 1970s demonstrated a technological pragmatism in keeping with the limited budgets of new nations, and responded positively to environmental concerns. Pre-fabricated building systems used by Americans (so as to accelerate the construction of various support facilities) during the Vietnam War were absorbed by the regional building industry.[17] Reinforced concrete components or concrete blocks, vertical and horizontal panels and lattices, sun shading devices and pragmatic uses of ornamentation were an integral part of the Modernist architectural vocabulary. Bold formal expression suppressed the colonial metropolitan identities that had dominated and shaped Asian cities for the past century, but more importantly, the choice of a neutral aesthetic for a nationalist architecture had the important function of defusing inter-ethnic tensions.

Chhatrapati Shivaji Terminus (Victoria Terminus)
Mumbai (Bombay), India 1887.
Architect – Frederick Stevens.

Imperial Theatre, Balangoda,
Sabaragamuwa, Sri Lanka.

Opposite Kandasamy House
Colombo, Sri Lanka 1999
Architect – Hiranti Weladawe

The unguarded universalism of the post-independent
period changed radically following the 1973 oil crisis,
when nations were forced to become self-reliant. It
also precipitated a cultural crisis fuelled by growing
disenchantment with Western-educated political elites
who had conceived a cosmopolitan psyche for their
nations. Chauvinistic nationalism, which manifested
itself in a revival of traditional building types, was now
projected as an architecture derived from and for the
people. Using colonial eclecticism as its model, the
nationalist state reproduced traditional architectural
forms at a monumental scale, using them to communicate its growing authority and power. The specific
religious and cultural characteristics of this traditionalist
approach precluded the existing cultural diversity of
postcolonial contexts. It promoted the culture of the
majority, and marginalised ethnic minorities.

The task facing a new generation of local architects
in the post-independence era was one of constructing
a sense of belonging against this former history of
colonial expression, utopian Modernism and its
counterpart of chauvinistic nationalism. In their
resolution of a postcolonial subjectivity split between
Europe and Asia, identity was conflated with geography and modernity was abstracted into climate-
driven responses. The architecture that evolved from

this approach was considered democratic, free of the
impediments of Westernisation, colonial class structure,
race and religion. The challenge posed to local architects was one of reconciling their Western design
training with designs for tropical environments. This
position resonated with architects in Malaysia and
later in Singapore, the youngest of the Southeast Asian
nations, which following independence in 1965 had
embarked on an unprecedented journey of progressive
nationalism. Singapore's anti-historical quest for *tabula
rasa* conditions was couched in the global rhetoric of
modernization. In Singapore, Modernism was developed
as part of a Malayan identity by the Malayan Architects
Co-Partnership, which aimed at deliberately
contextualizing the global aesthetic through climatic
responses. William Lim, Ken Yeang, and Tay Kheng
Soon would subsequently develop this approach as a
self-conscious Tropical Modernist agenda, which would
be used to define each project. The scope of this agenda,
influenced by Japanese Metabolist experiments and
by the technological change in their own economy,
would increasingly be applied to urban solutions.

It is important to recognize the significance of climate
in the construction of new architectural forms and
experience. In the search for identity through architecture, climate as an approach appeared to be both

inclusive and innocuous, and yet able to accommodate the key tenets of Modernism. Attention to local regional variations was used to define particular communities within national boundaries, while climate was also used to claim more general regional alliances. Through climate, the once colonized territories of South and Southeast Asia could reclaim their common history and forge a geographical identity as a vast regional landscape spanning three oceans. As developing nations struggling to gain attention in the global marketplace, this collective identity gave the region a substantial presence. The 'tropical' could be read as anti-colonial, anti-traditionalist and anti-International Style, "an architecture of resistance", as observed by Kenneth Frampton.[18] It would re-direct the architectural discourse on Modernism towards a post-modern interpretation of vernacular architecture.

A CONTEMPORARY VERNACULAR

In his foreword to *Contemporary Vernacular: Evoking Traditions in Asian Architecture*, prominent Indian architect Charles Correa framed the vernacular approach as a contemporary use of tradition.[19] Citing the organic and social processes implicit in the term 'vernacular', Correa's interpretation, and indeed that of the two authors of the volume, Tan Hock Beng and William Lim, addressed the inevitable schism faced by a professional practice straddling modernity and tradition. Although the organic and societal dimensions of this approach were absent from the houses for a wealthy Asian clientele featured in their book, it celebrated Asia's twenty year romance with vernacular ideals. The rhetoric that underwrote the vernacular approach, and its emphasis on traditions, both in building practice and cultural habits, originated in a moral economy particular to regions where the poverty of the rural agrarian population demanded appropriate technological solutions.

The technologies appropriate for developing countries were the recurring story line of the *Mimar* journals produced from 1981 to 1992 under the auspices of the Aga Khan Foundation. The foundation took on the imperatives of the vernacular approach, promoting the works of its adherents in its monograph series and awarding annual accolades to architects who contributed to community architecture. Although primarily focused on Islamic communities and countries, this preference was not exclusive to the foundation's objectives. Low-cost technologies, 'architecture without architects', and buildings that reinforced community identities were given an equal platform with the projects of individual professionals. In education, the centres for research shifted from England to North America, where Aga Khan programmes at Harvard and MIT trained professionals from non-Western countries in design research.

In Asia, the vernacular approach had its largest audience in the subcontinent, where, due to the vastness of India's geography and its large population, traditional patterns of agriculture, community and building practice persisted despite colonial intervention. While modernity as a political and social concept had influenced this population in numerous ways, it had failed to alleviate the burden of everyday life. Architects whose social conscience had led them to address such economic conditions, found that the easiest solution was a pragmatic architecture, which required little or no specialization. For architects disinterested in such social programmes, the rural vernacular provided an idealistic platform from which to build a sense of geographic belonging for an urban population who, through sustained interactions with colonial culture, had been alienated from their traditional roots.

The Festival of India (1983-86) organized by the Indian government and held in Britain, France and Japan generated a new awareness of architecture as an indigenous tradition. Its architectural exhibition, *Vistara*, invoked indigenous themes, traditionally neglected vernacular architecture, and buildings from the colonial era. This was an unconventional pluralistic approach.[20] Charles Correa and Ashish Ganju were involved in its manifesto, which placed their own architectural agendas at the centre of a discourse on Indian identity. Indian architecture was presented as a series of epiphanies where the various historic epochs, including the Vedic, Islamic and British colonial periods were presented as a succession of myths or paradigm shifts, and formalized Hindu structures were given mystical and metaphysical meanings.[21] The focus on local cultures that followed the Festival of India was encapsulated in craft museums, the village India complex and a reinvention of the vernacular. In Bombay, the centre of postmodern Indian culture, and with a ubiquitous colonial urban fabric, culture was reinterpreted as heritage conservation, and articulated through periodic urban festivals. Thus throughout the 1980s in South Asia, it was the bazaar and the village that took on the burden of identity production.

While a rising craft consciousness paved the way for India's contemporary vernacular, Sri Lanka's vernacular imagery was an interesting hybrid of both colonial and

18 K Frampton, "Towards a Critical Regionalism: Six points of an architecture of resistance" in H Foster (ed.), *The Anti-aesthetic: essays on postmodern culture*, Port Townsend, Washington: Bay Press, 1983, pp16-30.

19 W Lim and HB Tan, *Contemporary vernacular: evoking traditions in Asian architecture*, Singapore: Select Books, 1998, pp10-11.

20 R Bhatt and S Bafna, "Post-Colonial Narratives of Indian Architecture", *Architecture+Design*, Vol XII, 6, Nov-Dec 1995, pp85-89.

21 Ibid.

22 A Boyd, "Houses by the Road", *The Ceylon Observer Pictorial*, 1939.

23 M De Silva, *The Life and Work of an Asian Woman Architect*, Colombo: Smart Media Productions,1998.

Opposite Yantra House
Auroville, India 1999
Architect – Poppo Pingel

24 R Powell, *Ken Yeang : rethinking the environmental filter*, Singapore: Landmark Books, 1989, p15.

25 The term Critical Regionalism referred to Lewis Mumford's discussions of a humane regional architecture and was used by Tzonis et al. in a discussion of architecture in the USA focusing on the change towards self-reflexive social commentaries during the 1960's. See A Tzonis, L Lefaivre, R Diamond, *Architecture in North America since 1960*, London: Thames and Hudson, 1995. Its relevance to the tropics has been discussed in details in A Tzonis, L Lefaivre, and B Stagno (eds.) *Tropical architecture: Critical regionalism in the age of globalization*. Chichester: Wiley-Academy, with Fonds, Prince Claus Fund for Culture and Development, The Netherlands, 2001, pp1-14.

26 Tzonis et al, 2001, p8. Kenneth Frampton, in a seminal essay on postmodern culture, reinterpreted this process of de-familiarization as producing a 'contextual modernism' that could resist the forces of universalization. See K Frampton, "Towards a Critical Regionalism: Six points of an architecture of resistance" in H Foster (ed.), *The Anti-aesthetic: essays on postmodern culture*, Port Townsend, Washington: Bay Press, 1983, pp16-30. The arguments of these authors drew on concurrent philosophies: the critical theory of the Frankfurt School, Victor Shklovsky's ideas of de-familiarization and phenomenological explorations of place-based experience.

27 The National Congress of Architecture, Indonesia, 1982, in Kusno, 2000, p181.

28 Regional Seminar in the series 'Exploring Architecture in Islamic Cultures' sponsored by the Aga Khan Award for Architecture, Universiti Teknologi Malaysia and Ministry of Culture Youth and Sports, Malaysia, held in Kuala Lumpur, Malaysia, 25-27 July 1983.

29 Kusno, 2000.

30 'Tropical Encounter Conference' held in San Jose, Costa Rica, in November 1998.

31 A seminar was held in 1995 by the AA Asia group in Singapore and hosted by Kerry Hill Architects. Neo Tropicality, The Tropical Workshop Series at National

indigenous traditions. Initiated by a study of 'houses by the road' by British architect Andrew Boyd, it focussed on the rhythm of tiled roof forms as an appropriate poetic for its architecture.[22] The deep-eaved veranda and the steep pitched roof were both essentialised as the primary characteristics of a Sri Lankan tradition. In the writing and work of Minette de Silva, the AA's first Asian woman architect, the Sri Lankan vernacular was framed as a way of building – following the tradition of small rural structures to be found all over the island.[23] Geoffrey Bawa embraced and developed this approach as his primary architectural idiom.

In India and Sri Lanka, the preference for the vernacular was formed during a lengthy period of socialist policies that effectively halted the supply of imported building materials. Local architects proved their ingenuity by utilizing local materials in innovative ways, which was most easily done using vernacular methods. The *Mimar* monographs of the 1980s are a testament to this process. They featured Geoffrey Bawa (Sri Lanka), and Charles Correa and Raj Rawal (India) in a gallery of non-Western architects who embraced the vernacular. Yet vernacular technologies could not be successfully transferred into large-scale modern commercial programmes, due to the scale associated with the type and its light-weight materials. This technological leap had to be attempted in Southeast Asia by 'tropical regionalism'.

CRITICAL REGIONALISM

The use of the term 'regional taxonomies' by Robert Powell[24] and his contemporaries in their discussions of Tropical Modernism was symptomatic of a period from the 1970s to the early 1990s, when social agendas and Structuralist methodologies began to influence architectural research. The study of building typologies, urban morphology, collage and the kit of parts approach to building construction were conceived as part of the 'grammar' of architecture. By the late 1990s, deconstruction had taken these meta-narratives apart, making diverse approaches to architectural analysis tenable. Textuality, rhetoric, reflexivity, and schizophrenia were among the many approaches used to open up the architectural discourse of a newly unified Europe in a Post-Modern/Post Structuralist scrutiny of aesthetic representation. In Asian contexts, largely untroubled by post-industrial melancholia, these ravages into the interior landscape of the architectural psyche had little impact. The struggle remained as one of constructing identity through phenomenological experience. It was

through this imaginary, based on common climatic experience and a reciprocal vernacular architecture that tropical architecture continued to be essentialised.

By the 1980s, the entire tropical belt of Asia had been de-colonised as independent republics. This gave the region a tenuous and, in many ways, amorphous identity based on climatic experience. Lacking any other physical or political logic, climate became the source of a regional identity, with architecture as its referent. Each separate country within ASEAN could fit its vernacular architecture and its kit of parts into a regional taxonomy, and derive an architecture that was clearly related to its cultural position. Modernist reinterpretation of this same vernacular would prevent its collapse into specific identities, while 'climate' held the entire discourse together. As argued by Tzonis, Lefaivre and Stagno, it constituted a 'Critical Regionalism', distinguishable from other forms of regionalism due to "its capability to create a renewed, versus an atavistic, sense of place in our time."[25] They contrasted it to Romantic Regionalism, which depended on familiar associations arousing "affinity" and "sympathy" in the viewer.[26]

The regionalist debate had its greatest audience in Southeast Asia, where rapid globalization posed a threat to national cultures derived from the rural vernacular. These nations had shared a water-based Melanesian culture, where the house on stilts and the boat-shaped dwelling recurred as images of a primitive architecture. Unlike in South Asia, where the vernacular was part of the everyday landscape, urbanization and affluence was relegating the vernacular to Southeast Asia's remote rural communities and urban poor. In successive forums held in Indonesia[27] and Malaysia,[28] the issue of regional identities was unravelled. Yet apart from its role in identity construction, the rural house-form was largely an artefact that would be eventually abandoned to development. Its fate had been predicted in the 'Beautiful Indonesia in Miniature Park' (1971), a Disney-type theme park built by the Suharto government outside Jakarta, in which the nation was represented as a colourful and harmonious village.[29] In Singapore, the *kampong* house gradually disappeared, leaving only the Chinese shophouse as an urban vernacular form. In Malaysia and Indonesia, the rural house type informed particular cultural institutions until, with rising religious tensions, these too were replaced by Middle–Eastern Islamic models. For the vernacular to have meaning for these booming Asian economies, tropical regionalism had to become an object of consumption.

A MODERNIST CRITIQUE

By the mid-1990's, Tropical Regionalism was the most pervasive architectural idiom to be disseminated throughout Asia through publishing, advertising and architectural production. The shift to Asia was corroborated by a series of workshops held at National University of Singapore, engaging practitioners who addressed the climatic agenda. Following a revival of the conference tradition in Costa Rica in1998[30] the International Conference on Tropical Architecture was resumed as a tradition, and was held in Singapore in 2004. It seemed that the discourse on tropical architecture would henceforth be firmly lodged on home turf.

The impetus of the 1990s revival of the tropical paradigm differed radically from its 1950s Modernist counterpart due to its translation via the vernacular. This change was most visible in a residential return to Southeast Asian rural typologies, evident in the use of pitched roofs and the introduction of ornamental ponds and pools adjacent to the houses. Following seminars held on this topic in Singapore, these house types were discussed in terms of the "contemporary vernacular" and "neo-tropicality".[31] The buildings that had been marginalized as temporary, primitive and impoverished were rapidly transformed into leading icons of a discourse on identity-formation. It produced only two distinctive types: the luxurious tropical house; and the tourist resort – additive buildings designed as clustered pavilion forms, which could successfully maintain the scale of vernacular structures. Framed as refuges from the gritty realities of Asian urban life, and as temporal rustic retreats, these models were mini utopias projecting an idyllic lifestyle in a tropical climate. Designed for wealthy businessmen, European expatriates or multinational resort chains, these resorts delivered a new product for the dollar economy within developing countries, and included the local labour. The dollar economy paid for exquisite detailing, creating a resurgence in local craft traditions and a boom in local materials. It produced high standards of design unaffordable to local clients. Its consumers were a Westernised elite and Western tourists who, unaware of the irony of its transformation, envisioned the tropical experience as an extension of a moment of colonization. The local had truly become global.

Viewed in retrospect, the significance of Tropical Regionalism and its inherent value had been in its ability to bring local identities into focus. From the late 1980s to the mid-1990s the regionalist discourse, riding on the wave of the Asian economic boom, changed the course of history by producing alternative

Peoples Park Complex, Singapore 1973. Architect – Design Partnership

democratic identities for modern Asians. It created a heritage industry that fed conservation and tourism, and generated new forms of environmental awareness. It gave new meaning to everyday spaces and practices, and it extended the life of everyday objects by transforming them into cultural icons for general consumption. The impact of a regional vernacular had an undeniable force in forging new confidence in the Asian region, and in the final years of the 20th Century it contributed to a coherent national discourse on architecture, perhaps the last of its kind, before rapid urbanization shifted architectural production to diverse autonomous practices.[32]

Despite its many successes, the tropical vernacular continued to use labour intensive construction methods based on colonial construction materials and processes. Its exploded programmes depleted valuable resources such as terracotta and timber, and exploited poorly paid local construction workers.[33] Subject to the inequities of a postcolonial class structure, the modest vernacular beginnings of the tropical vernacular were thus subsumed by the bid to commodify, reproduce and market the tropical experience. Given the alternative of its idyllic template, few Asian architects proved willing to

University of Singapore 2001 was led by Chan Soo Khian. Both events addressed issues of the contemporary vernacular and neo-tropicalism.

32 Kusno, 2000, p181.

33 "... in 1978, there were some 3,000 recognized brick kilns in Sri Lanka alone, each producing an average 150,000 bricks a year, sufficient to build over 50,000 houses. But not without cost to the consumer, and a heavy one to the environment: a firing of 25,000 bricks can consume forty forest trees, a rate of deforestation in Sri Lanka alone of around 750,000 trees a year." See P Oliver, *Dwellings: The House across the World*, Oxford: Phaidon, 1987, p104 (in reference to Robson, Gormley & Sonawane, *Aided Self-help Housing in Sri Lanka 1977-1982*, Report for Overseas Development Administration, London, 1984)

Opposite: The Arris
Apartments, Singapore 2003.
Architect – W Architects

abandon climatic imperatives in favour of the pressing social agendas of a developing nation. Consequently in the past two decades many Asian designers turned their backs on modern technologies, modular systems, lightweight materials or methods of easy assemblage that might deliver low-cost housing to its population. In this respect, and unlike Australia or America, they did not contribute to the creation of a large home-owning middle-class or deliver equitable spaces or building practices that confronted feudal or colonial asymmetries within homes or institutions. Tropical Regionalism proved to be an inadequate register of the radical transformations of its host contexts and the cosmopolitan Asian subjectivities that were then emerging.

AN EMERGING COSMOPOLITANISM

By the end of the 20th Century, the tropical paradigm was limited to a few programmatic typologies. Openings for diversity were, however, created outside this phenomenon as new localized forms of an emerging cosmopolitan modernity. This new focus projected 21st Century Asia as a region that has embraced monetization with development as its objective. Its architectural icons were monolithic shopping malls, soaring office towers and the twisted ribbons of urban expressways. These new urban symbols force confrontation with a very different, often dystopian, vision of an urban Asian subject who is differentiated by race, class and gender, and is caught in a storm of economic liberalization. The region's globalization can be read in architectural firms and at building sites, as increasing numbers of migrants, women, and expatriates swell local practices. Modernity in Asia is inscribed on the female subject, whose entry into the public sphere has provoked progressive policies as well as a cultural crisis. Such adjustments and displacements should precipitate changes in the architectural programme whether at home or at work. In the face of these transformations, the discourse on the tropical vernacular has reached its natural limit as clients and users find its scale and aesthetic inappropriate for the complex programmes of contemporary life. More importantly, the rhetoric of identity, which has long supported the climatic position, has run its course and no longer serves its original postcolonial purpose. With rapid urbanization Asians too will become more receptive to 'home-grown' forms of modernity and more confident in their manipulation.

As the focus of architectural debates swings from tradition to modernity, the fluctuations unwittingly reflect problems faced by professionals who confront the virulent politics and crony capitalism of the region. As observed by Tay Kheng Soon, "Architects of the Third World must develop a thorough understanding of the nature of power and the political process, for only then can their projects be deeply relevant and historically significant".[34] The lack of an architectural consciousness or healthy debate on public architecture is symptomatic of a profession where many architects are desperate to build while clients and contractors have scant interest in their intellectual positions. During the Asian recession, the tendency to filter big projects through established practices with political connections has aggravated the economic plight of many small design firms. Moreover, the tremendous impact of globalization filtered through East Asia needs to be acknowledged as one of the many intellectual blind spots of Asian regionalist discourse.

The history of architectural change during the 20th Century traced the transformation of Asians from colonial and national subjects to producers and consumers of modern identities in a post-modern world. Peculiar to this transformation is the 'split subjectivity' described by Homi Bhaba,[35] the mixed loyalties, and creolized identities that straddle both Europe and Asia, all symptomatic of a postcolonial condition. As modern Asian people blend strong filial connections and meaningful cultural traditions with economic aspirations and cosmopolitan desires, they will produce a material culture quite unlike that found elsewhere. Political imperatives, economic necessity and cultural practices such as geomancy, religious belief and familial relations, have undone the utopian expectations of both Modernism and Regionalism: proving the inadequacy of purely functional, tectonic or climatic responses.

Particular to the region has been its resilience to its own hybrid history, and its ability to absorb and maintain contradictory versions of its self within the same architectural template. In Western social theory, it is evidence of the schizophrenia that accompanies the flexible accumulation of capital and labour across both traditional and modern cultural realities.[36] Indeed it is Tropical Asia's ability to transform modern imperatives to suit its own ideological frameworks that makes its architecture exciting and different. In the post-national era, the new Asian citizen has left the dappled light of the tropical verandah for the reflected light of the shopping mall, the muted glow of the video arcade and the neon flicker of the city street. But how have the region's architects begun to programme, conceptualise, and design for this future? The works in this book go far in answering this question.

34 KS Tay, *Exploring Architecture in Islamic Cultures 1: Architecture and Identity*, The Aga Khan Awards for Architecture, Singapore: Concept Media, 1983, p49.

35 Bhaba, 1994, p38.

36 In reference to the ideas of G Deleuze and F Guattari, *A thousand plateaus: capitalism and schizophrenia*, London: Athlone Press, 1988, 1987; and F Jameson *Postmodernism of the Logic of the Late Capitalism*, Durham: Duke University Press, 1991.

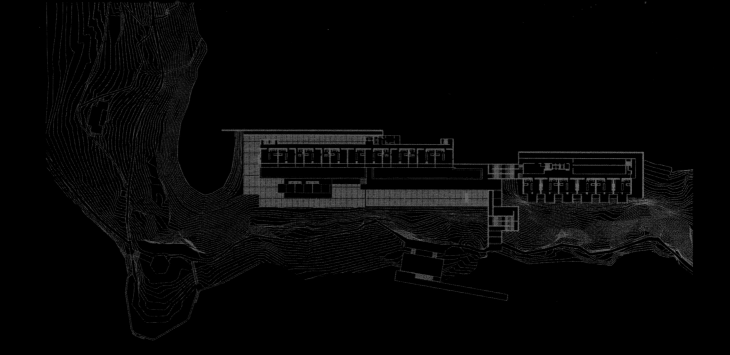

Kerry Hill

Kerry Hill (born Perth, Australia, 1943) studied at the Perth
Technical College and the University of Western Australia,
graduating in 1968. He worked for Howlett & Bailey in Perth
from 1969 to 1971 before leaving Australia to work in Hong
Kong and Bali for Hong Kong-based architects/engineers
Palmer & Turner from 1972 until 1974. From 1974 to 1978 he
managed the Palmer & Turner office in Jakarta. He
established Kerry Hill Architects in Singapore in 1979. Hill
has lectured at the National University of Singapore, the
University of Hawaii, the University of Western Australia and
the University of Queensland. His work has been exhibited
in Perth. Important completed projects include The Darwin
Performing Arts Centre, Darwin, Australia (1986); The
Heritage, Brisbane, Australia (1989); The Sukhothai, Bangkok,
Thailand (1991); The Sentosa, Singapore (1991); Amanusa
Hotel, Nusa Dua, Bali (1992); The Chedi, Bandung, Indonesia
(1993); The Datai, Pulau Langkawi, Malaysia (1993); The Serai,
Manggis, Bali (1994); Australian High Commissioner's
Residence, Singapore (1996); Genesis, Singapore (1997); Cluny
Hill House, Singapore (1997); Ooi House, Margaret River,
Western Australia (1997); Ceylinco Seylan Towers, Colombo
(1998); Cricket Pavilion, Singapore Cricket Association,
Singapore (1999); Mirzan House, Kuala Lumpur, Malaysia
(1999); Ogilvie House, Sunshine Beach, Queensland, Australia
(2002); The Lalu, Sun Moon Lake, Taiwan (2002); Amansara,
Siem Reap, Cambodia (2003); Sonar Bangla Hotel, Kolkata
(2003); and Zoo Entry, Singapore Zoo (2003). He received the
1995 Kenneth F Brown Asia Pacific Culture and Architecture
Design Award, the 2001 Aga Khan Award for Architecture
and the 2003 RAIA Robin Boyd Award for the Ogilvie House.
His work has been published in A+U (Japan), Architectural
Digest, Hauser (Germany), Architectural Review, Wallpaper,
World Architecture (UK), Architecture Australia, Monument
(Australia), Indian Architect & Builder (India), Singapore
Architect and Space (Singapore).

Essay and project descriptions by Philip Goad

"My own reading has centred on materiality, and the intrinsic value of one material paying respect to another. This, combined with a pervasive sense of spatial order, is the lesson I have carried elsewhere."

There can be few contemporary architects who have sustained more than thirty years of hotel design, and who have continued to refine their design approach so that each new hotel provides surprise, invention and accomplished spatial and experiential theatre. In tropical Asia, the pre-eminent practitioner of this art is Kerry Hill. While critics swoop on resort architectures as embodying simulacra of the authentic – exquisite and exotic 'other worldly' escapes for the privileged few – the proof of Hill's architecture denies such narrow criticism. His ability to sensitively reinterpret traditional spatial and formal types, and to respond appropriately to place, transcends the cliché. And in recent works, Hill's independence from debased regionalism (often the result of resort architecture's dalliance with the vernacular) has been further secured. With The Lalu, Sun Moon Lake, Taiwan (2002) and Sonar Bangla, Calcutta (2003), Hill shows a decisive move – away from recasting recognisable typologies to a higher level of abstraction and refinement of detail. This strategy reinforces the design strengths which have always underpinned Hill's architecture: a rigorously orchestrated sequence of arrival, reception and spatial release, based around themes of axis, court and framed view. The discipline of elemental repetition, a symmetry without cloying cliché, the siting of blank walls to shift direction and the eye, and an intention that has visual repose as its goal, cumulatively engender a Zen-like calm to Hill's work. The success of this approach, especially in Hill's hotel designs, is the consistency of the language of parts developed for each project. All are a measure of the thoroughness of an original intention driven home by plan, section, form, detail and exquisite complementary landscaping. In compositional terms, Hill's designs parallel works by venerable planimetric architect/artists such as Ludwig Mies van der Rohe, Louis Kahn, Tadao Ando and Craig Ellwood. A key difference is Kerry Hill's formal deployment of the courtyard as a key element of tropical design: for psychological containment; for borrowing shade from walls rather than obvious roofs; for spatial expansion to frame views or vertical connection with the sky; for retreat from the relative chaos of the city without; for the courtyard's ability to cross-ventilate between spaces; and for the opportunity to allow water or plants to provide visual relief and contemplation. The court (or series of courts) combined with floating flat roofs, enables edges to be blurred. Whole walls can disappear, and magical tropical existence, half-inside and half-outside, whether in sun or rain, becomes possible.

The success of Hill's architecture derives from more than three decades of intense work in the region. A major influence was his time as site architect on the Bali Hyatt, Sanur (1972-73) when he came in contact with Geoffrey Bawa and Peter Muller, the two architects who set the boutique hotel scene on its global regionalist course with their pioneering work in Sri Lanka and Bali in the late 1970s and early 1980s. But Hill's early independent works like Amanusa, Bali (1992),

The Chedi, Bandung (1993), The Datai, Pulau Langkawi (1993), and The Serai, Bali (1994) escape the romantic artlessness of Muller and Bawa's work, moving towards more polished, controlled, even monumental, conceptions of what the hotel might be. It is as if, for Hill, the hotel were a testing ground for broader conceptions of what a civic architecture for tropical Asia might entail. In this, Hill has been assisted by his twenty-six-year association with Javanese-born Dutch national Adrian Zecha, who later founded the Aman resort chain. In working for Aman, Hill has had, and continues to have, a sympathetic client with similar aims.

Kerry Hill's practice is not limited to hotel commissions. Some of his firm's most interesting works are either one-off detached houses or commercial projects located within urban centres. In three Singapore projects, for example, Hill uses the timber-slatted screen as a multi-functioning device, suggesting another element to include in a tropical architectural grammar. At the Genesis office building (1997), the screen becomes a giant urban façade, a permeable skin that suggests an alternative to the pervasive anonymity and ubiquity of Singapore's hermetic glazed curtain walls. At the Singapore Cricket Club pavilion (1999), the timber screen is a pragmatic lightweight infill between flat base and flat roof, while at the Singapore Zoo (2003), the timber screen is not just placed vertically in a variety of syncopated patterns, but in the horizontal dimension (as a roof) in contrast to long walls of stone. The slatted screen becomes a wonderful, almost fragile, pergola; softening the light and softening the transition to a dramatic skillion roof. Timber is also used underfoot, and a timber deck studded with log columns acts as a tactile signal of threshold before the zoo experience. Here one sees Hill realise a statement made with respect to his hotel architecture: "My own reading has centred on materiality, and the intrinsic value of one material paying respect to another. This, combined with a pervasive sense of spatial order, is the lesson I have carried elsewhere."

Indeed, Hill's lesson is carried to intense levels in individual house designs, where he deploys the techniques that characterise his resort and urban projects. In the Ooi House, Western Australia (1997), the Mirzan House, Kuala Lumpur (1999) and the Ogilvie House, Australia (2002), Hill combines the ideas of court, timber-slatted screen, the framed panorama, the calming presence of water against mass, and a rigorous spatial order. In short, Hill captures the serenity of each place, each site and its landscape in the contained project of the single dwelling. In the tropical Asian (and Australasian) context, such tranquillity is a rare and hard-fought prize. This is the distinctive aspect of Kerry Hill's practice, and the key to his role as mentor to a generation of architects who have passed through his office. Hill's practice is based in Singapore, but his work is located across the globe – a place-based practice that is now touching the world.

The Lalu

Year of completion 2002
Location Sun Moon Lake, Taiwan
Architect Kerry Hill

Below The idea of 'screen' affects every element of The Lalu, from the design of lamps to the modulation of a gridded ceiling.

Opposite The timber porte cochere: an essay in repetition and precision. Kerry Hill is at pains to emphasis the persistence of craft as an indicator of place and tradition.

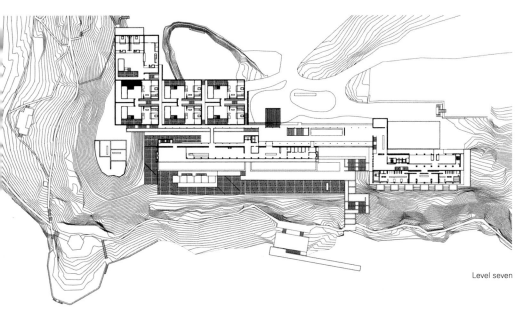

Level seven

The beautiful and historic setting for The Lalu, Taiwan's first international five-star hotel, is the Lalu Peninsula on the famous Sun Moon Lake in the nation's central region. The lake is of special significance to the Taiwanese for its associations as the site of the indigenous Shao aboriginal settlement, and for the Japanese, the location is significant for their occupation during World War II. Both the Japanese royal family and the first president of Taiwan, Chiang Kai Shek, had summer palaces here, and the history of the ten-hectare site as a resort location dates from 1901. In completing the project, the original Chinese palace-style building was renovated and two new buildings were designed by Kerry Hill to complement the original villa as well as the greater landscape. In a typically Zen-like response, Hill decided to focus on simplifying his working palette to a series of four major building materials: wood, stone, glass and steel. As a result, each part of the hotel highlights, with ultimate precision, the qualities and potential of each material. The screens and posts are built from timber, stone appears as the ground plane and as vertical piers, while steel is used as a complementary delineating line in support of timber and glass. As with the Singapore Zoo project, The Lalu is a meditation on the Modernist goals of simplicity through reduction. But, like much of the tradition of building in Asia, those special buildings which require timber construction are treated with reverence and absolute respect for how each element joins, meets, and collaborates with another. As with the Sonar Bangla in Kolkata, The Lalu belongs to its site, though instead of courtyard containment, this hotel embraces its picturesque setting. The Lalu invites every hotel guest to take part in its wonderful scene, and be witness to both the sun and the moon.

Below and opposite left
At the hotel's main entrance, Kerry Hill employs timber as a screening element in both the horizontal and vertical dimensions. The half shade softens and accentuates the warmth of the material, a contemporary echo of Taiwan's timber villa and temple traditions.

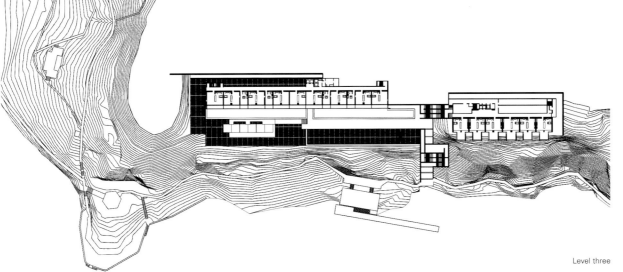

Level three

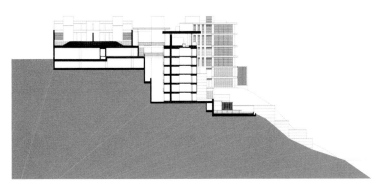

Section

Opposite Against the landscape, the screened canopies and steel posts seem to engage in equal dialogue, but also as built datum points. They delineate the organic, often serpentine line of the mountains behind.

Below The main block of The Lalu faces the lake like a giant viewing screen, above a long lap pool which acts like an ornamental reflecting pool. The rooms and the roof terrace all face the panorama. Nature is celebrated as the focus of mental regeneration and reflection.

Ogilvie House

Year of completion 2003
Location Sunshine Beach, Queensland, Australia
Architect Kerry Hill

The Ogilvie House is unlike any other contemporary house in sub-tropical Queensland. It doesn't adopt the usual local palette of corrugated iron, fly-away roof and excited appendages of shading devices. Its pedigree appears to lie more within Kerry Hill's recent shedding of iconic vernacular moments and his emphasis on the abstract, fundamental components of controlled spatial sequence, the casting of deep shade through emphatic horizontal roofs and timber screens at the very edges of his forms, and the continuous deployment of the courtyard as a self-shading mechanism. With a dream-like vista overlooking a surf-beach, this house – containing spacious family living quarters, a caretaker's unit, car parking, a home-office, and a gallery for the owner's collection of Australian art – is organised around a masterful visual and spatial sequence of terraced garden, decks, living spaces and pools stepping down the sloping site. Flanking these spaces are, in the tradition of Louis Kahn, service and functional zones, which effectively form private 'walls' to the open spaces between, and provide the architectural frame for a spectacular view of azure sea and pellucid sky beyond. The horizon becomes a critical datum in a composition of changing floor and water levels. Entry is from the lowest part of the site and one enters the house unsuspecting of the spatial drama about to unfold. One enters a large entrance hall before a reflection pool, unaware of the bank of three bedrooms, each with ensuite, to one's right. Shifting axis left, and after passing through the gallery, one arrives upstairs at the very centre of the house with a view across to a lower deck and a swimming pool whose edge melts into the ocean. Echoing the rigorously formalist plans of such American architects as Craig Ellwood, Pierre Koenig and Eliot Noyes in the 1950s, and applying Kerry Hill's relentless ascetic precision, the Ogilvie House is a faultless exercise in defining a possible language for domestic serenity.

Opposite Seen from below, the eastern façade of the house reads as a series of sliding timber screens. The depth of the first floor swimming pool is concealed within the projecting block of bedrooms.

Above The heart of the house is the pool terrace, separated from the living room by a sunken courtyard. Beyond the pool is the client's home office: a spectacular setting for work, with views of Sunshine Beach and the Pacific Ocean.

Left The view from the living room: the flanking bedroom and office wings frame a spectacular ocean view across the timber pool deck. Kerry Hill's recognized skill in planning the reception spaces of resort hotels – using water and the framing of a panoramic view – is evidenced here with the creation of a magnificent ever-changing painting of water, cloud and sky.

Right Above the screened verandah, which conceals the depth of the swimming pool, the client's home office can be seen in the foreground, and the master bedroom suite lies beyond. This is an alternative form of verandah in the Queensland tradition, with sliding screens that open on to the eastern lawn, looking over two terraced levels to the beach.

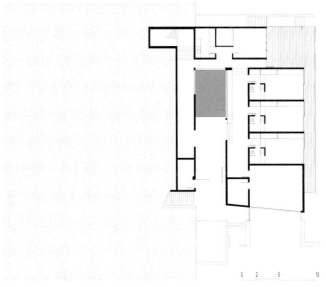

0   2   5   10

Lower level

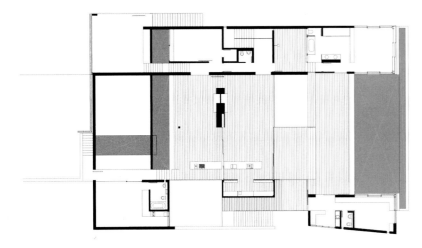

Upper level

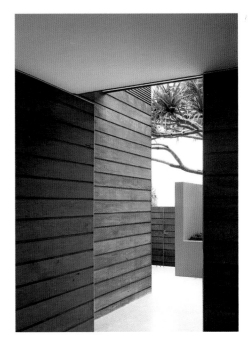

Left The guest room corridor is not so much a passage, but a picture gallery with pieces from the owner's collection of Australian contemporary art. To the left is the sunken pool court, the entry hall and another picture gallery beyond.

Above The discreet entry from the street steps around an existing pandanus tree.

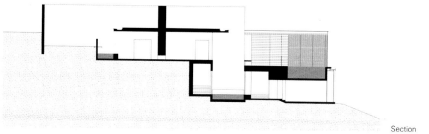

Section

Entrance Plaza, Singapore Zoological Gardens

Year of completion 2003
Location Singapore
Architect Kerry Hill

Right Kerry Hill uses the slatted timber ceiling beneath a glass roof as a major linking element in this De Stijl piece of urban design.

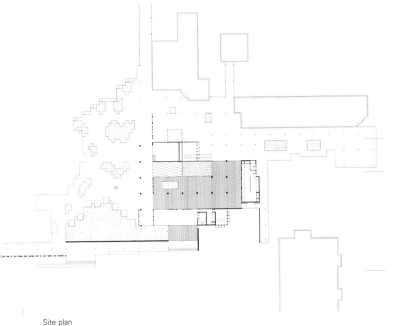

Site plan

The Singapore Zoo is one of the country's most popular tourist attractions, with visitors arriving by bus, car and taxi in huge numbers at all times of the day. Thus the entry sequence is critical, not just to the operating efficiency of the complex, but also to the orientation before entry into the gardens. In designing a new series of buildings to mark the entry, and to provide ticketing, retail and café spaces, Kerry Hill took advantage of the circulation problem to define asymmetrical axes that pinwheel into the arrival landscape. Textured stone-faced fin walls, flat canopies and repetitive banks of vertical 'sticks' track endlessly off at right angles to each other, defining the various drop-off routes for each mode of transport. The exception to this orthogonal reverie is the skillion roof before the main courtyard, with giant white lettering attached to a vertical Balau timber screen. Part of the roof to the main gathering area is finished with a lowered 'ceiling' of timber battens that filters the sunlight: one feels as if one is in the ever-changing half-light of shade cast by trees, and underneath one's feet the floor surface also changes, with timber decking consisting of railway-sized Balau sleepers. The oversized circular columns are also clad in Balau timber, and the Zoo insisted that only certified plantation timbers were to be used, all sourced from Sabah in East Malaysia. With this skilful piece of almost 'pure' architecture, Hill has combined existing buildings and added discreet new box forms beneath a masterful play of planar and screened roofs. In essence, he has made tactile the virtues of De Stijl planning: wall, floor, ceiling and supports are all enlisted in a celebration of abstract space and material pleasure.

Left Beneath a glazed roof is a timber slatted ceiling which casts a myriad of striated shadows across the timber floor of the main space of the entry court. This view looks back to the main traffic drop off point.

Sonar Bangla Hotel

Year of completion 2003
Location Kolkata, India
Architect Kerry Hill

Not since the days of the Raj has there been a hotel like the Sonar Bangla in Kolkata. With its level of finish and detail, its inclusion of huge water bodies, and in its palatial ambience, this complex will set new standards for boutique hotel architecture in contemporary India. From the futuristic flaring white concrete entry canopy, a tour through the hotel seems to be a glimpse into the future: there is a feeling of another world. There is a backward glance to Edward Durrell Stone's New Delhi architecture of the 1950s, and even further back to the exuberant 17th century Moghul architecture, but instead of drawing on colonial references or mimicking the refurbishment of a maharaja's palace, Kerry Hill has produced a contemporary building with the grandeur and quality of a Moghul emperor's water garden. The Sonar Bangla is furnished with an architecture of measured elegance, with filigrees of timber and terra cotta screens, and constantly imbued with the reflective calm of water, made subtly fluid with the changing light of the day. References have been made to the *bagaanbari*, the garden houses or pleasure retreats built by Bengal zaminders (landowners) on the outskirts of the city, and the calm muted restraint of the building's finish and layout recalls those villas of a bygone era. Overlooking one of the greenest areas of Kolkata, the grounds of Sona Bangla occupy over 15 acres. Three guest blocks, two high-rise blocks and one low-rise block provide 231 five-star rooms, and with the reception, functions room and restaurant block, comprise the surrounding faces of a vast courtyard entirely filled with water. This space is an immense lily pond, punctuated only by a few floating palms and a series of meditation pavilions: smaller, more private versions of the much larger projecting pavilion that houses the axial highlight of the lobby lounge. Kerry Hill demonstrates his finesse at re-describing place – this time Kolkata – holding up a new building as a mirror to its location and making fresh discoveries. At Sonar Bangla, Hill has used the program of the hotel – one of travel and itinerancy – and has strangely found himself summarising the essence of a city's multi-faceted spatial psyche.

Left Looking across a lily pond towards the vast entry court to the hotel, one has a sense of arriving at a palatial compound. Blank walls, huge oversailing eaves and the graceful centre point of the white colonnade of flaring canopies set a tone of ceremony and luxury.

Opposite The hotel opens onto a huge water garden. The western low-rise bank of guest rooms overlooks this sea of tranquillity, as does the high-rise block of superior suites beyond. Guest lounges sit within the pond like floating temples or pleasure pavilions.

Opposite The main lounge, below the reception area, overlooks the central lily pond and courtyard. Light is filtered through a block-work grille on three sides of this double height space: a hint, on a grander public scale, of the diminutive jewel-like pavilions beyond.

Below Sitting within a vast arrival court, the extraordinary free standing porte-cochere is an exuberant formal contrast to the dominant palette of stone, terracotta and timber.

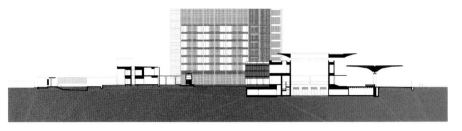

Section

Right A guests' lounge is dark and secluded, with a plush colour scheme of deep reds and browns: a refuge from the heat and glare of Kolkata.

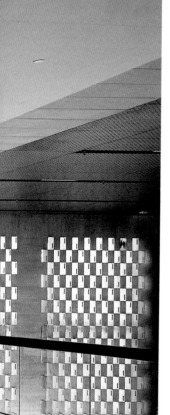

Left and right Repetition and contrast characterize Kerry Hill's material choices. The reflective materials of glass and stone are used internally to form a bright airy contrast to the rich material tones outside.

Below Kerry Hill's use of terracotta and timber is a unique interpretation of local Bengali material traditions. Combined with water, his simplified abstract forms cross centuries in mood and evocation.

Right Looking east towards the main lounge across the lily pond. The use of timber and terracotta as screening devices soften the prismatic forms.

Opposite View across the central lily pond to the main lounge near reception. In the foreground, is one of the 'floating' guest lounges. Detailed timber screens in Moghul-inspired patterns offer privacy, while small fountains play softly across the expanse of the pool.

Level two

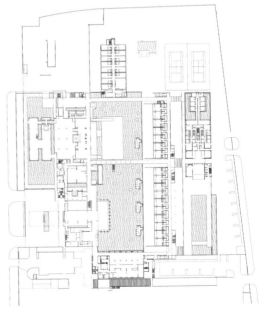

Level one

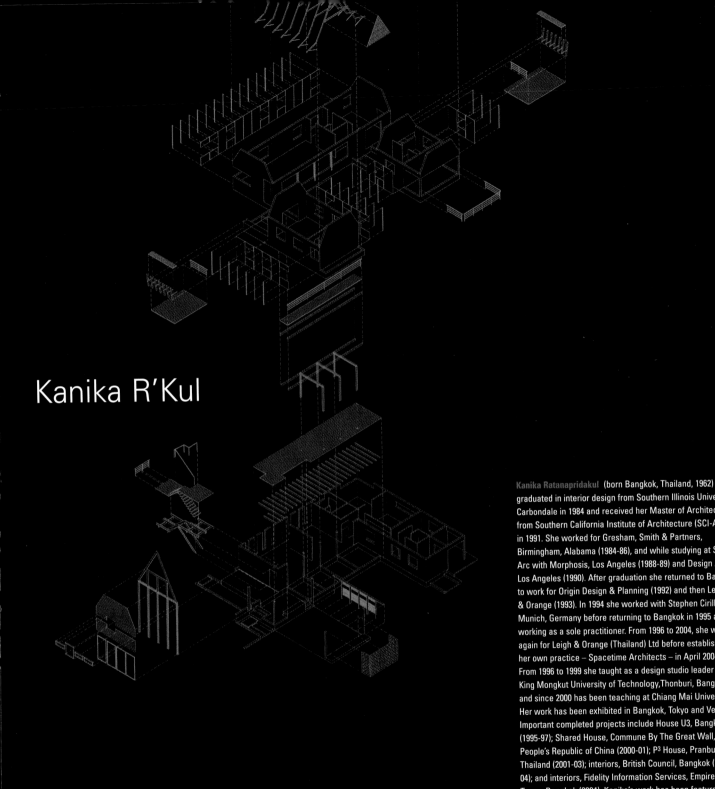

Kanika R'Kul

Essay and project descriptions by Philip Goad

Kanika Ratanapridakul (born Bangkok, Thailand, 1962) graduated in interior design from Southern Illinois University, Carbondale in 1984 and received her Master of Architecture from Southern California Institute of Architecture (SCI-Arc) in 1991. She worked for Gresham, Smith & Partners, Birmingham, Alabama (1984-86), and while studying at SCI-Arc with Morphosis, Los Angeles (1988-89) and Design Atelier, Los Angeles (1990). After graduation she returned to Bangkok to work for Origin Design & Planning (1992) and then Leigh & Orange (1993). In 1994 she worked with Stephen Cirillo in Munich, Germany before returning to Bangkok in 1995 and working as a sole practitioner. From 1996 to 2004, she worked again for Leigh & Orange (Thailand) Ltd before establishing her own practice – Spacetime Architects – in April 2004. From 1996 to 1999 she taught as a design studio leader at King Mongkut University of Technology,Thonburi, Bangkok, and since 2000 has been teaching at Chiang Mai University. Her work has been exhibited in Bangkok, Tokyo and Venice. Important completed projects include House U3, Bangkok (1995-97); Shared House, Commune By The Great Wall, People's Republic of China (2000-01); P³ House, Pranburi, Thailand (2001-03); interiors, British Council, Bangkok (2003-04); and interiors, Fidelity Information Services, Empire Tower, Bangkok (2004). Kanika's work has been featured in numerous journals including art4d (Thailand), A+U (Japan), Asian Interior Design (Spain), House and Garden (Thailand), Monument (Australia), Scale: New China issue (Thailand), Singapore Architect (Singapore), and World Architecture (UK), ASA (Thailand) and Hinge (Hong Kong).

Kanika Ratanapridakul is not overly interested in the nature of 'tropical', but is fascinated by the nature of the Asian city – its grain, fabric and morphology.

The buildings of Thai architect Kanika R'kul are modest in size and number, but intense in content. Her way of working is emblematic of a new possibility for practice in tropical Asia – especially at the level of the small scale – with an ethic of employing humble means to achieve higher social, intellectual and experiential goals. "How to be useful" is Kanika's career maxim. It is for her a constant and consuming question.

Though Kanika herself, with typical self-deprecation, denies any deliberate intention to create a specifically modern Thai idiom – this is what her architecture has come to represent – possibly by default. For example, House U3 (1995-97), in suburban Bangkok, was intended to be a simple exercise: resolving the domestic requirements of an extended family, and providing acoustic and spatial independence, privacy and shaded outdoor space. Typical subdivision plot dimensions were analysed and steep gable roofs to shed monsoon rain were used. These roofs appear to, though deliberately do not, echo the traditional Thai house. As a result, Kanika's architecture feeds directly into the development of a contemporary sensibility for Thai architecture, but not through grand symbolic narratives or a signature personal idiom. It occurs through an intimate engagement with function and interior as the site of rewriting some of architecture's generic habits. Inadvertently, this approach struck a chord with colleagues and commentators on contemporary Thai architecture, those struggling to find identity amidst Thailand's eager embrace of the West and a perceived loss of local architectural identity.

Initially trained in the USA as an interior designer and then as an architect, Kanika points to formative influences from that experience. As a student, she briefly experienced the rigorous formalism of the Los Angeles firm of Morphosis, led by Michael Rotondi, and this was followed by the studios she took at SCI-Arc with such architects as Robert Mangurian, Wolf Prix, Meryl Elam and Lars Lerup, where the process of model-making and learning to work with materials such as aluminium and fibreglass alerted her to the discipline of 'making', and the need to be more systematic with materials. Kanika has thus developed a system or rule with her material choices. This keeps builders in check, and it guides more inventive material choices; hence her enjoyment, for example, of the modular qualities of off-the-shelf fibre-cement sheet. Another important SCI-Arc influence was Joan Copjec, former editor of the journal October, whose theory class instilled in Kanika the importance of the politics of representation and the need to de-school, re-learn and define for herself an ethical politic for architectural practice.

On returning to Thailand in 1992, departing again in 1994 and finally returning in 1995, Kanika found that she was 'reintroduced' to Thailand. She found that the perspective of her overseas education and her attachment to Bangkok and her family heightened the sense of critical distance from deeply ingrained local habits and fashionable modes of practice. Kanika found, to her good fortune, that she was intellectually removed, and therefore free to develop her own ideas.

Working for Leigh & Orange from 1995 gave her the opportunity to work on interesting, well funded projects from a small office environment. Kanika's Shared House for the Commune By The Great Wall at the Shui Guan mountain range, near Beijing (2000-01) enabled an exploration of the shared or public spaces of a home and a deliberate strategy of not replicating Western typologies or that of the Chinese courtyard house. Her interiors for the British Council in Bangkok at Siam Square (2001) and Ladprao Centre (2003-04) allowed inexpensive experiments with moulded plywood, doughnut-shaped seats and fundamental spatial exercises with simple shapes that paralleled the 1950s phenomenological experiments of Dutch architect Aldo van Eyck. In the Fidelity Information Services office fitout (2004), clear and white panels of glass become the guiding system. One of the hallmarks of Kanika's practice is "travelling light": celebrating flexibility (she detests over-designed interiors) and leaving materials in their natural state. She is not overly interested in the nature of 'tropical', but instead is fascinated by the nature of the Asian city – its grain, fabric and morphology.

The P3 House at Pranburi (2001-03) gains its name from three P's: coastal Pranburi with its winds and urban face; Perpendicular for the dominant vertical rhythms; and Parallel for the spatial strategy applied to the site. For Kanika, it represents another system to be followed. With the Prosper office building project (2004), a similar tripartite system is followed, and for the Third House, Bangkok (2004-), a house for a mother, daughter and son is another series of three parallel slivers. In many of her projects, Kanika develops a linear volume or atrium space: it is sometimes external, sometimes internal; it can be public, and it can be a private verandah; it can also be a cross-ventilating passage… or indeed, all of these.

In April 2004, Kanika formed her own practice – Space Time – in a refurbished warehouse building in Bangkok. She also teaches at Chiang Mai University, 'giving back' as she describes it; investing in the next generation of Thai architects. This is, for her, part of 'being useful'. Despite being educated outside Thailand, she is intensely interested in the future of Thai architecture. This is a chance to, in the most humble way, affect change not through personal achievement but subtly and generously through others, sharing her knowledge and inspiring others, so that a new sense of "Thai-ness" might emerge. As she reflected in Singapore Architect (212):

"Now – the only tiny problem I have to face is how to make it all happen. Because I realise that, given the track record, it will be quite a task. But Thai people do possess an incredible ability to adapt, improvise and smile at all cost – a true survival instinct.

So – One step at a time – I suppose."

House U3

Year of completion 1997
Location Bangkok, Thailand
Architect Kanika R'Kul

West elevation

Above The steep roof profile with its upturned edge has earned praises for its unselfconscious Thai evocation. The broad entry verandah becomes a front porch, a meeting point for the family, and where the stair rises up to the separate living areas.

Opposite At the first floor level, the verandah becomes a public street, expanding into private/public terraces. To the right is Kanika's sister's wing, and beyond is Kanika's studio/loft clad in fibre cement sheet.

When Kanika R'kul's parents decided to build a new house, it was an opportunity for her family to come together on the suburban site in Bangkok on which she and her sister had grown up. House U3 is a residence for the whole family, but with independent living quarters for Kanika, her sister and her parents, with a separate building housing the kitchen and service areas. It is, in effect, a complex of two storey buildings bound together by the common public space of an intercommunicating verandah on both levels. This gesture of providing a public space – a gap – between the various private lives of each suite of rooms is a favoured tactic for Kanika. This space also acts as a ventilating element, allowing the various buildings to breathe, as if the house were a miniature village. The structure of House U3 is a concrete frame with rendered blockwork infill, and there are two extra 'skins' over the blockwork on the western façade: vertical fibre cement sheets denote Kanika's studio-loft, while a horizontal timber battened screen provides shade for her sister's apartment. This screen supplies a lighter evocation of structure, in keeping with the delicate roof profiles of each pavilion. Designed with intense regard to prevailing breezes and sun angles, and with a dramatically pitched roof to shed rainwater quickly, the resulting form of this house suggests a refreshing new paradigm for the contemporary Thai house.

Level one

Level two

Shared House

Year of completion 2001
Location Commune By The Great Wall, Shui Guan,
People's Republic of China
Architect Kanika R'Kul

The Commune By The Great Wall is a unique project, where a series of houses have been designed by some of the world's most progressive young architects in a spectacular landscape of forested hills near the Great Wall at Badaling, fifty kilometers northwest of Beijing. The Great Wall can be seen running along the ridges above the houses, and in this context Kanika's contribution can be seen as a rumination on the public and private spaces of domestic life. Outdoor terraces on the three levels become public piazze, and a sky-lit internal gallery space on the first floor becomes a public street between the bedrooms and bathing areas. A narrow double-height stair volume becomes a dramatic alleyway between the 'buildings' of space and at ground level it terminates as a glazed sitting bay. Externally this volume reads as a built promontory, in effect, it is the house's own 'great wall'. A graphic square of timber battens across the centre of the long glass face of the ground floor living rooms becomes an oversized screen, a sign in the larger landscape, and a way of modulating the internal space behind. With this house, Kanika has not attempted formal, structural or tectonic gymnastics but has instead taken the route of a calm meditation on the nature of a few key ideas about dwelling, monumentality and landscape. This measured position does indicate reticence, but shrewd judgement on the scale and significance of the historic and monumental context of the landscape.

Above The double-height stair hall slices through the plan, its narrow vertical space is like an urban alleyway.

Right A composition of walls and terraces on a slope beneath the Great Wall: this house reads at a variety of scales from afar. The huge timber screen, almost square, denotes a vast area of living spaces behind.

Below The emphasised volume of the double height stair hall creates a glazed bay-window space at ground level and a rooftop architectural promontory, to gain full prospect of the spectacular surrounding landscape.

Opposite The theme of public space in the Shared House takes the form of a series of outdoor terraces and stairs: it is as if one is traversing the similar landscape of stairs, terraces and ramps of the Great Wall.

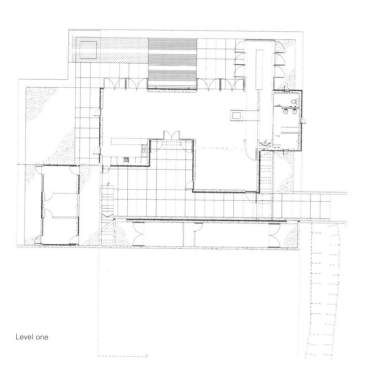

Level one

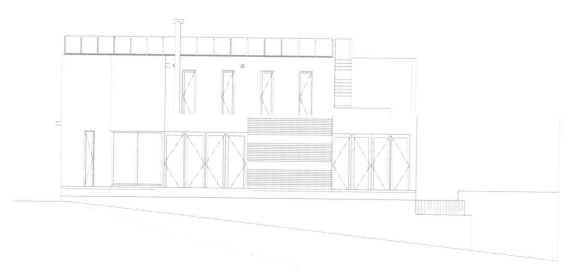

North elevation

Below Inside the stair hall, a battened timber screen diffuses the glare. It hangs like a permanent curtain.

Opposite Looking down the stair one has an axial vista to the 'light' and to the landscape beyond. To the left is the 'dark' volume of the upper passage.

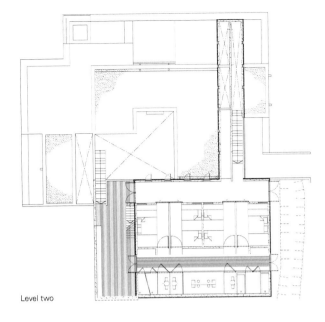

Level two

P³ House

Year of completion 2003
Location Pranburi, Prachuabkhirikhan, Thailand
Architect Kanika R'Kul

Opposite From the beach, the house appears tall: reading as a composition of horizontals against the verticals of the native pines within and behind it. This is the private face of the house but public in the sense that it gives itself completely over to the view.

Below The shared verandah at upper level opens up to sweeping views of the gulf of Thailand and the beautiful white sands of Pran Buri beach.

Dotted with the wonderfully tall trunks of native pine trees, the site for this weekend retreat at Pranburi is right on the beach, and the proportions of the house appear to have been borrowed from this setting. When viewed from the beach, the house, with a restrained grey and predominantly perpendicular palette of unpainted cement render, generous glazing, unfinished fibre cement sheet, fin walls, and slender timber and concrete posts, seems to merge into the landscape. Built with a limited budget, the house is divided in two: the main house and the guest quarters are separated by a broad timber deck between two parallel fin walls, which passes from the entry of the house straight through to the line of the horizon above the ocean. This deck is one of Kanika's public streets inserted into a domestic setting, and this time it is an axis to infinity. The two 'houses'

are joined above by a common roof-deck; this is another public space, but an elevated one, which also covers the long slice of the entry 'gap' below. The two 'houses' thus come together through a concept of shared public space. There is another reflection on notions of public and private: the semi-solid street face of the house is deliberately private, clad in fibre cement sheet with timber cover strips and small-scaled window openings. By contrast, the expression of the seaside façade is transparency, as if the occupants are taking part in the public landscape of the beach, and in the public space of the greater landscape of the sea and its sky.

Left The living space with
its minimal material palette:
timber, cement render and
polished concrete floors.
Beyond is the timber deck,
the house's 'public street'.

Opposite The street-side
façade of the house has
a broad timber deck as
its focus. This deck slices
the house in two, and
emphasises the composition
as one of parallel lines and
perpendicular junctions.
Above is the shared roof
deck: the house's elevated
'piazza'.

Lower level

Upper level

Roof level

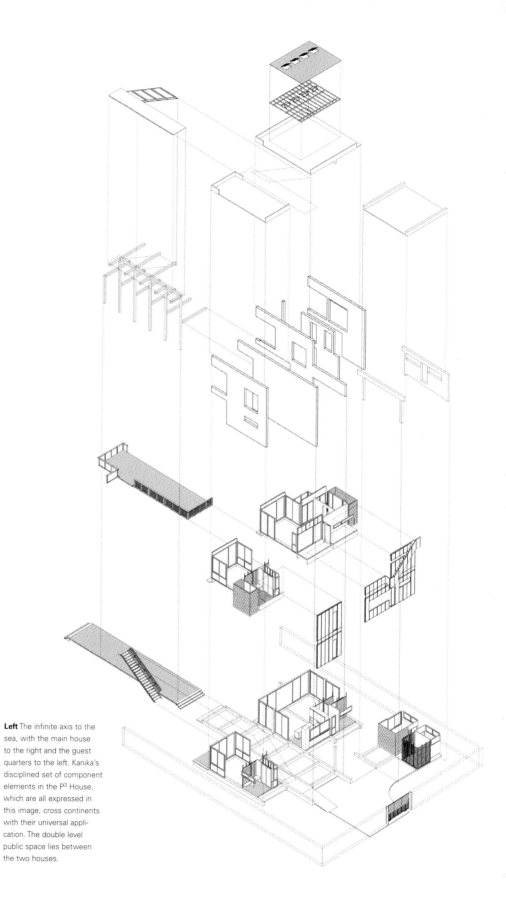

Left The infinite axis to the sea, with the main house to the right and the guest quarters to the left. Kanika's disciplined set of component elements in the P³ House, which are all expressed in this image, cross continents with their universal application. The double level public space lies between the two houses.

Cheong Yew Kuan (born Kuantan, Malaysia, 1962) graduated from the National University of Singapore in 1988. As a student he worked for William Lim Associates in Singapore (1986-88) and from August 1988 until August 1994 with Kerry Hill Architects. In 1994 he established his own practice, Area Designs, which is based in Singapore and Bali. Important completed projects include the Hardy House, Baung, Bali, Indonesia (1994-96); Begawan Giri Estate, Bali, Indonesia (1994-99); Dharmawangsar Hotel, Jakarta, Indonesia (1993-96); House A, Batujimbar, Bali, Indonesia (1998-99); Chris Gentry House, Sayan, Bali, Indonesia (1998-2000); Courtyard House, Bali, Indonesia (1998-2003); Four Seasons Residences, Jimbaran, Bali, Indonesia (1999-2001); Williams-Hillier houses, Pabean, Bali, Indonesia (2000-02); Parrot Cay Spa, Turks and Caicos Islands (2001-03); Santo House, Jimbaran, Bali, Indonesia (2002-04); Cocoa Beach Resort, Maldives (2002-03); and Umaparo, Bhutan (2001-04). Kuan's buildings have been published in *Architectural Digest* (USA), *Vogue Living, Elle Décor* and *Houses for the 21st Century,* Periplus (2003).

Essay and project descriptions by Philip Goad

... in building for himself, Cheong Yew Kuan was able to finally depart from tradition and fully develop his appreciation for Balinese space.

In an economic climate that feeds upon uncontrolled growth, quick financial turnaround and rampant globalization, a decision to not take part in such a process might be considered radical. But for Malaysian-born architect Cheong Yew Kuan, that isn't really the question. His decision has been to accept the variable 'slowness' of his place of practice, be it Bali, Indonesia or even fast-paced Singapore. Kuan takes the position, as he describes it, of a chef who uses ingredients that are seasonal and appropriate to place. For a chef, these are natural and accepted limits. And Kuan believes architecture is like that – local and place-dependent. He has no wish to have a practice that is too large, hence out of his control. He simply wants to build well.

This carefully considered position on practice has been gradually acquired by Kuan, and six years in the Singapore office of Kerry Hill taught him a great deal. He worked on resort designs such as the golf-course buildings for Amanusa at Nusa Dua, Bali, and on other resort projects in Singapore, Jakarta and Vietnam, and with other talented young colleagues like Richard Hassell and Wong Mun Summ (the future directors of WOHA). He learnt how to build and how to achieve control over the various design elements at his disposal, especially spatial sequence and the archi- tectonic frame. But it was a commission that originally came into the Hill office, and which over time gradually became his own, that formed the most instructive design laboratory for Kuan's personal development.

Bradley Gardner's initial concept, in 1990, for the Begawan Giri was a series of holiday houses overlooking a spectacular gorge north of Ubud. But by 1994, when Kuan had set up practice in Singapore, the scheme had evolved dramatically, and the Begawan Giri had become his own project. It had become a resort, and Kuan moved to Bali to oversee its design and construction. Yet in many ways, the commission had no formal structure or final brief, and its relaxed ad-hoc nature meant that each guest villa was an experiment in a different architectural idea. Each villa was not obviously Balinese, but every one of the five houses was designed in harmony with local traditions and sited with meticulous care.

During the drawn-out construction process of Begawan Giri (1994-99), Kuan found that his own design had become freer, departing from certain rules. He developed a design approach for himself, at odds with the conspicuous over-achievement and aggressive 'borrowing' of Singapore's architectural culture. Kuan's first independently gained commission, the Hardy House, Sayan (1994-96) consolidated that new found freedom. It was an intensely crafted tree-house folly, beautifully sited and demanding intimate engagement with its clients, a fine art jeweller and his wife, but simultaneously, Kuan was working hard to escape the power of the local Balinese context. Unlike the highly wrought interpretations of traditional Balinese architecture which had emanated from designers such as Peter Muller and, to a lesser degree Kerry Hill, Kuan opted for a more robust, almost primitive idiom – massive timber columns, areas of cement-rendered mass and heavy thatched roofs. The Hardy House, the Begawan Giri guest villas, the Jimbaran estate villas (1999-2001), the Chris Gentry House, Sanur (1998-2000) and the Michelle Han House, Sanur (1999) were thus exercises in working through a primeval language of archetypes. Kuan also developed a local knowledge of construction, and collected around him a small group of trusted contractors.

Kuan's intellectual breakthrough was in the design for his own house and office – the Courtyard House (1998-2003). Importantly, in building for himself and acting as contractor, Kuan was able to finally depart from tradition and fully develop his appreciation for Balinese space, especially the courtyard and the ritualistic organization of houses and temples, whilst also employing his palette of archetypal elements of post and beam, and broad expanses of unadorned walls. In a flat rice-paddy landscape near the sea, the Williams-Hillier House, near Gianyar, Bali (2000-02) adopted the pavilion planning of the Balinese house compound, but the gable roof profiles, the giant concrete frame and flat roofed connecting galleries have no local precedent. On a dramatic and dry hill-side site in Jimbaran, the Santo House (2002-04) takes its visual cues from the curvilinear P&O streamlined styling of Indonesian 1950s Modernism. Each of these house designs is different – different clients, different construction and different material practices. And for Kuan, context is critical – a commission is "never a blank piece of paper".

After ten years of working in Bali, Cheong Yew Kuan continues to be concerned with moving on from pre-determined forms – but in a slow way. He is not particularly interested in another 'rustic' house, but he feels that the forms of Modernism are so homo- geneous and ubiquitous that few places around the globe are capable of an authentic architectural evolution arising directly from their location. For him, people have to "reacclimatize". This has been one of the most valuable lessons contained within the recent and complex desire for resort architecture – a return to the basics of body, food and revitalisation. While many of Kuan's clients can be counted among the world's wealthy and famous – he has commissions across the globe, in the Caribbean, Maldives, Bhutan and Madagascar – he understands that his responsibility is, in essence, a fundamental one: to provide an appropriate, even humble, framework for living.

Begawan Giri

Location Begawan, Bali, Indonesia
Date 1999
Architect Cheong Yew Kuan

Below The pool and living terrace of 'Tejasuara' (sound of fire). Beneath the traditional thatched roof is the villa's main living space. To the right, in pavilions constructed of huge logs, are the sleeping quarters and stone steps that lead to the villa's front entry gate.

Opposite The forms of 'Wanakasa' (forest in the mist), roofed in shingles, perch in the tree tops above a series of terraces and steps engraved in the landscape.

Site plan

Now one of Bali's most exclusive resorts, Begawan Giri – "wise man's mountain" – was the brainchild of Bradley Gardner, built as a series of five exquisitely designed and sited villas perched on the impossibly steep slopes, gullies and ridges of the Ayung River gorge. Much of the site was replanted and re-landscaped with meandering stone paths, terrace walls and pockets of hidden lawn. Each house has been positioned so that absolute privacy is assured, and one feels that there is your villa, the jungle, and nothing else. Each house was designed around a separate elemental theme such as earth, wind, water, fire and mist, and Cheong Yew Kuan's aim was to neutralise the cliched Balinese house reproductions typical of much resort architecture, and to search for architectural fundamentals. Begawan Giri was Kuan's six-year Bali 'design laboratory': its seamless completion is a testament to the vision and persistence of its architect and client.

Hardy House

Year of completion 1996
Location Baung, Bali, Indonesia
Architect Cheong Yew Kuan

On a spectacular site overlooking the Ayung River gorge, this house is a fantasy of craft, a gloriously indulgent and magical primitive hut. One arrives at the entrance to this house before a massive adobe wall with huge carved timber gates draped by the vines of a massive tree. Open the gates and the surprise is palpable: across the garden and a reflective pool, sits a two-storey house, with a completely open living platform and a glazed-in kitchen. It's as if the residents live inside a giant picture frame, and everyday existence becomes the setting of a real-life painting. Out of view is the service wing, concealed by adobe walls and thatched roofs, and a mysterious winding mud-brick tunnel leading to the garage.

A close examination of the main house, reveals that its structure is an eminently rational frame, made visually complex by the addition of carefully sourced natural log props as well as three diagonal timber struts, which stabilise the tall portal structure.

Cheong Yew Kuan is rather wistful about this house, his first independent commission. For him, it holds many of the vestiges of the sheer romance of Bali; its ability as a place to become paradise, and as a setting to realise some of the most fundamental aspects of dwelling. But visible here are the bones of an elemental architecture that now guide his current design practice.

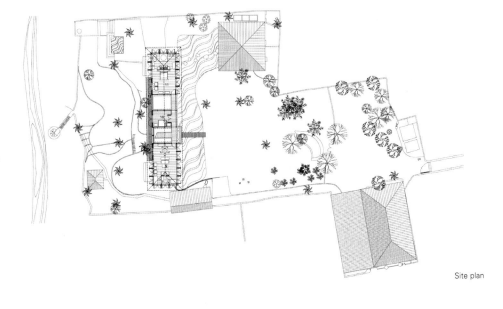

Site plan

Above The main living space, entirely open, feels like a platform amongst tree trunks. Here the clear structural simplicity of the frame is given artful 'nature' by the inclusion of diagonal log props.

Opposite Stepping-stones lead across a reflecting pool to the living platform. Above, a balustrade, inside the line of open windows, becomes another series in the multiple series of sticks that comprise this sophisticated tree house.

Section

Williams-Hillier House

Year of completion 2002
Location Pabean, Bali, Indonesia
Architect Cheong Yew Kuan

On a one-hectare site, slightly elevated above the sea near Gianyar on the southern coast of Bali, these two houses have been designed for two sisters and their families. The site, once grazing land, has a series of mature coconut palms dotted throughout the garden. Spatially, the complex is an expanded version of the compound setting of a traditional Balinese house: there are two gable-roofed houses, a guest pavilion, and an entertainment *bale* pavilion overlooking the main swimming pool. Each of the houses reads as an independent long pavilion, one of which is roofed by an 'eccentric' gable which dips lower on its verandah side to give greater sun protection, and beneath these contemporary interpretations of the Balinese roof, each of the house's living spaces can be completely opened to the elements. The distinctive component of these houses is the supporting concrete frame: giant post and beam portals that signify contemporary, even primal, interpretations of local construction archetypes. With the masterful siting of these two houses and in their detail and structural delineation, Cheong Yew Kuan satisfies his clients, long-time visitors and residents of Bali, who were 'over' the traditional Balinese house but still were in awe of its ability to encompass a tranquillity and spatial repose missing from an urban lifestyle.

Site plan

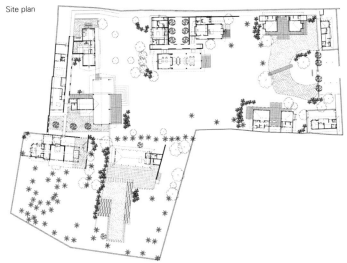

Section

Above Flat concrete
canopies provide protected
walkways and serve as
galleries to both houses.
They also become shading
devices, separated from the
main gabled living space by
a reflecting pool. The thick
mats on the floor act as
giant stepping-stones.

Santo House

Year of completion 2004
Location Jimbaran, Bali, Indonesia
Architect Cheong Yew Kuan

Perched atop a hill, looking across the lower slopes of the Bukit peninsula between Jimbaran and Nusa Dua, the Santo House is an unexpected discovery within an estate of pseudo-Balinese contemporary villas. While the conventional hipped roofs bow to the inevitable pressures of neighbourhood context, the rest of the house portrays a decidedly different character. The chief architectural gesture is a startling, almost expressionistic, curving concrete balcony that sweeps the length of the living pavilion to join the sleeping pavilion, a three-storey block angled away to embrace the swimming pool below.

The style of the house is deliberately non-Balinese, echoing the 1950s P&O style streamlining favoured during the Suharto years, a yearning for a nascent modernity, which has since given way to the power of regionalist forms and detail ubiquitous in Bali. The bold abstract painted forms below the roofline reflect the independent spirit of the house's owner, whose unusual collection of giant pieces of petrified timber form sculptural groupings in the entry and courtyard garden. The Santo House reveals Cheong Yew Kuan's responsiveness to a specific client and place: it's all eminently down-to-earth, but the house is skirted by a wild curving balustrade and joyously coloured walls which refuse to acknowledge the sentimentality of the neighbourhood's instant patina of age.

Right Beneath the dynamic curve of the upstairs northern verandah are the playroom, family room and a covered outdoor terrace.

Opposite As if inserting the Corbusian recipe of *pilotis* and a free plan into the section of a traditional Dutch Colonial house form, the Santo House is an expressionistic hybrid – Hans Scharoun in the tropics!

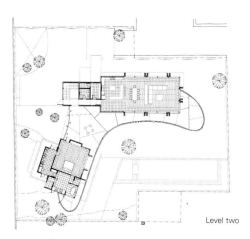

Level two

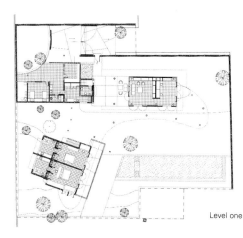

Level one

Courtyard House

Year of completion 2003
Location Bali, Indonesia
Architect Cheong Yew Kuan

Right Roll-down blinds provide the only enclosing element to the living and dining space. Cheong Yew Kuan's lamps and daybed are modest additions to this relaxed space, between the grass of the courtyard and the water of the pools – both natural 'floors' with a space of community between.

Designed by Cheong Yew Kuan for himself, with a studio-office attached, this house is a description of a post and beam frame deployed to create a series of flat roofed pavilions – some enclosed, some completely open – which in turn create a series of courtyards. The feeling of the house is utterly relaxed, as if Kuan has been able to ignore the visual preconceptions that one has of a building in Bali and has focused instead on the island's spatial and experiential magic. Kuan has also been able to indulge his love of furniture design, and the interior divulges his personality through calm, timeless pieces of elemental furniture – a day bed, cylindrical lamps, a stool made from a tree trunk. In building this modern house, Kuan wanted to anchor his building in local materials. In eventual frustration at not being able to procure the correct thickness of the original local clay bricks, he used the thinner contemporary equivalent as a wall cladding on

the series of enclosing walls, which emphasise one of Bali's special qualities – the pleasure of the threshold. One proceeds through a series of gateways, shifting axes, framed vistas, parallel paths – one solid, the other a lap pool – before finally reaching a climax in the west pavilion overlooking the river gorge. Here, as with the Hardy House's living frame, is a place for meditation, a sunken covered terrace where the lap pool appears to drift over into the gorge: one sits at the contemplative hinge point of the house, between the nurtured landscape of the courtyard and the wilderness beyond.

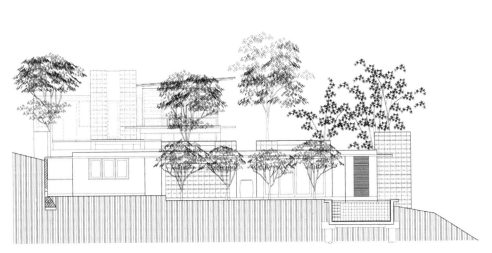

Section

Above Looking back along the lap pool to the living room and guest wing to the right, across the courtyard of ferns and frangipani. A relatively sparsely planted and 'furnished' courtyard: as with the traditional Balinese house compound, which was never over-planted.

Opposite The first threshold of the Courtyard House is a gap between two terracotta-clad walls. The vertical stones planted in the garden of the entry forecourt can be seen through the gap. The lily pond and the frangipani tree – 'site' and 'smell' – are centring elements in this first experience of the house.

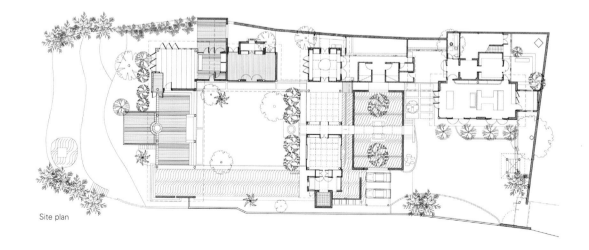

Site plan

Below A 'copse' of stones planted at the entry to the house.

Right Cheong Yew Kuan's furnishing of his living and dining terrace utilizes furniture and furnishings of his own design. Beyond, on axis, a circular table in the kitchen is made from the trunk of a massive tree. The simple framework of the concrete portal frame becomes the calm backdrop to this elegant indoor/outdoor space.

Left Arrival at the house occurs through a series of wall openings which frame the axis across the lily pond, through the house and over the garden courtyard to the view over the wilderness.

Right The outdoor living terrace conceals an alcove with a built-in couch. Here one is entirely removed from the rest of the house, on a terrace where one can potentially commune with nature and the gods.

Left A circular skylight in the off–form concrete ceiling, aligned with a vertical gap in the terracotta panelled walls above the lap pool, provides a meditative setting for the sunken terrace.

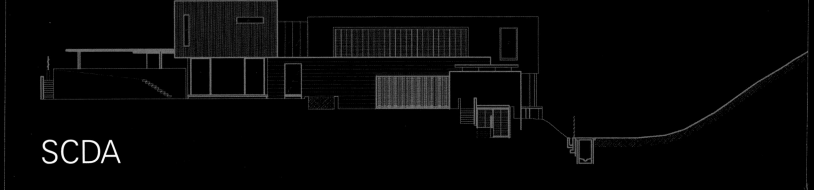

SCDA

Chan Soo Khian (born Penang, Malaysia, 1962) graduated
with a Bachelor of Arts from Washington University in 1984
and as Master of Architecture from Yale University in 1987.
After working for Allan Greenberg Architects from 1987 to
1988, for Kohn Pedersen Fox from 1988 to 1990, and then with
A61 in Singapore from 1990 to 1995, Chan established SCDA
Architects in Singapore in 1995. He opened a branch office in
Kuala Lumpur in 2003. He has taught at National University of
Singapore and at Syracuse University, New York. Important
completed projects include the Coronation Road West House,
Singapore (1998-2000); the masterplan and design of the Qing
Pu Development, Shanghai, People's Republic of China (2001);
the Andrew Road House, Singapore (2002); the Heeren
Shophouse, Melaka, Malaysia (2002); the Ladyhill apartments,
Singapore (2002); the Lincoln Modern apartments, Singapore
(2001-03); and the Dalvey Estate House, Singapore (2004).
The work of SCDA has been published in *Architectural
Record* (USA), *Architectural Review* (UK), *Lotus* (Italy),
Monument (Australia), and *World Architecture* (UK).

Essay and project descriptions by Philip Goad

Chan's talent has been to develop a distinctive interpretation of Modernism, emphasising horizontality through dramatic oversailing eaves, exaggerated stone coursing and hovering prismatic forms.

Chan Soo Khian is one of the new breed of Singapore architects – cosmopolitan, globally aware, overseas-educated, an elegant formalist, and with a practice base across the Southeast Asian region. He is ambitious not just for his own architecture but also for discourse within the region. His choice of the term 'Neo-Tropicality', for example, for the 2001 Tropical Workshop Series at the National University of Singapore, raised hackles amongst an older generation of architects who felt that such a term smacked of style, rather than research into the idea of what a socially responsible tropical architecture might mean; but Malaysian-born Chan shrugs off such comments, arguing that 'Neo-Tropicality' translates as a 'new' tropicality. He continues to make provocative statements and demonstrates his virtuoso design skills through active, commercially savvy, practice. Substantial one-off houses, apartment buildings and condominiums form the focus of SCDA, the practice he founded in 1995. And Chan can point to success through global peer recognition: the US journal Architectural Record nominated him as one of 2003's 'Design Vanguards', and he received the British journal Architectural Review's 'ar+d 2002' highly commended award for an emerging young architect; rare achievements for an architect from the region.

Much of the attention lavished on SCDA is due to Chan's compositional skills, influenced in large part by the rigours of his Yale University education, and his experience with Kohn Pedersen & Fox in the late 1980s: when that office was internationally renowned for sophisticated elemental and tectonic composition combined with material richness and conscientiously modulated surfaces. Chan's talent has been to develop a distinctive interpretation of Modernism, emphasising horizontality through dramatic oversailing eaves, exaggerated stone coursing and hovering prismatic forms. While the inspiration in formal juxtaposition would appear to be the early 20th Century experiments of the De Stijl architects and the sliding forms and plans of Ludwig Mies van der Rohe, the interest in material texture, colour and contrast suggests a corresponding material wealth to Chan's Singapore clientele. The villa-setting of the Andrew Road House (2002), for example, and its dramatic cantilevering parasol roof above a floating box form is the provocative challenge to the bourgeois mock-historic palaces favoured by Singapore's wealthy class. Similarly, the Coronation Road West House (1998-2000), though on a more constricted site close to the street, has its materials of stone and concrete and timber layered in the vertical dimension. It is a compressed version of the horizon-seeking planes of the unrestricted Andrew Road House. The Dalvey Estate House (2004) however takes both of these themes to the next level, a calmer, more severe juxtaposition of two simplified box forms creating a simple L-shaped division of a suburban site. The floating flat roof with

broad oversailing eaves has been discarded, and the scheme's uncompromising simplicity is suggestive of an emerging refinement to the highly wrought quality of SCDA's earlier residential commissions.

This shift towards a stronger definition of elemental units becomes evident when one compares the Ladyhill Condominiums, near Orchard Road in Singapore (2002) to the Lincoln Modern apartments (2003). The affluent neighbourhood near Orchard Road has dictated the restrained formal response and gracious scale of the apartment plans of Ladyhill. It is a luxuriant complex with a resort-style swimming pool and landscaping, demonstrating a preoccupation with surface richness, and a subtle gradation of the scales of transparency of glass, screen, wall and foliage. By contrast, Lincoln Modern is a bolder experiment in apartment typology – stylish *existenzminimum* Le Corbusier-inspired apartment designs that have two storey loft-like living spaces, which interlock up the height of the building. This interlocking arrangement of different sized apartments can be 'read' from afar, as can the various escape stairs and service cores. The extreme height and the narrow depth of the apartment block combine with bright orange fin details to produce a composition that echoes the high-rise visions of Iakov Chernikov, the Russian Constructivist. Such radical images from the past, which can suggest innovative ways of thinking about density and plan type in Singapore, seem possible within the range and scale of SCDA's work.

Perhaps this seed of vision is best expressed in one of SCDA's smallest projects, the insertion of a new house/pavilion within the walls of a Chinese shophouse in Melaka (2002). Here Chan's concerns for material richness are played up to their optimum level. His skill in composing the sharp-edged planes of a jewel-like pavilion box, and then placing it above a lap-pool within decaying water-stained and mildew encrusted walls, results in a sort of post-apocalyptic pleasure folly. Taken together, the qualities of SCDA's work – the material inclusions denoting wealth and luxury, the *sachlich* experiments in apartment type, and the poetic juxtaposition of the ultra-designed and the as-found – signal diverse new directions available to a concept of 'Neo-Tropicality'.

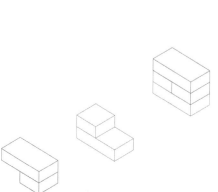
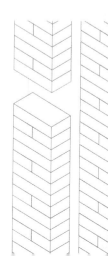

Heeren Shophouse

Year of completion 2002
Location Melaka, Malaysia
Architect SCDA

Located within a precinct of some of the finest historic buildings in Melaka, the Heeren Shophouse comprises the insertion of a meditation pavilion within the decaying shell of a ruined Chinese shophouse. The roof and floor had collapsed, and there was virtually nothing left inside the building's four walls. The typical shophouse has a very long narrow plan behind the ground-floor shop which opens directly onto an arcaded walkway on the street. The shopkeepers lived above the shop, and light and air entered the deep plans of these buildings through courtyards which occupied a substantial length of the sliver-like subdivision. SCDA retained the historic Heeren Street (now Jl Tun Tan Cheng Lock) façade, including the doors and timber screens, and stabilised the party walls, deliberately leaving them in their heavily weathered state. The idea was to celebrate the poignant and poetic contrast between old and new. Entry is still through the original front doors, a garden of planted bamboo is in place of the shop. Set far back into the depth of the site, the four rooms of the contemplation pavilion were designed as crisply detailed concrete and timber cubic forms, occupying the space of the courtyard volume of the original shop house, while the formerly occupied volumes of the shophouse have been left as voids. Rolled steel I-beams were used to brace the side walls, and these beams support a floating timber-battened box housing the sleeping spaces. At night, this structure glows like a lantern held aloft within the dark and moody length of the volume. Directly beneath the floating box, as if tracing its form on the ground, is a slender lap pool. In a poetic gesture, a swing hangs from one of the steel beams over the pool, imparting an eerie sense of forbidden pleasure. At the rear of the site, excavation created more open space, and enabled SCDA to project a meditation box as a cubic mass over a ruined wall. Beyond this, in a small courtyard is a vegetable garden, an orchard, septic tanks and solar panels. The conscientious retention of the patina of age is celebrated in the manner that 'pleasing decay' is highlighted within a traditional Chinese garden. The architectural, ornamental and structural ruins of a Chinese shophouse in Melaka become the equivalent of the aged beauty of a natural landscape, and are viewed from the modern version of a scholar's contemplation pavilion. Space, form, and nature have all been inverted to reflect on the history of another time and another world.

Left With a canoe beside the reflective pool, it is as if some traveller has come upon this pristine cavern in an urban wilderness. The 'lantern-like' meditation box is perched on a steel portal, which braces the decayed and weathered walls.

Opposite The view from the front door into the original shop, which is now a front garden planted with bamboo and overlooked by a new glazed and battened living space.

Below The meditation/sleeping box interior is like an architectural nest: a 'bower' softened by gossamer-like curtains.

Right The view from the old front rooms of the original shophouse, where a new spiral steel stair allows one to ascend to a new living space/platform. Very few changes have been made to the original structure, and this has been a deliberate strategy to highlight the disjuncture: the dialectic resonance between old and new.

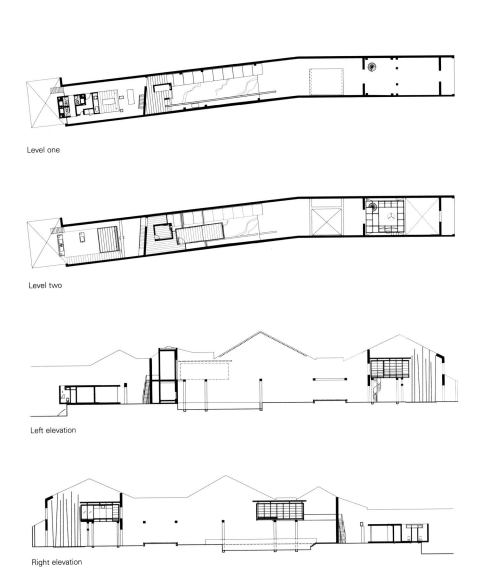

Level one

Level two

Left elevation

Right elevation

Coronation Road West House

Year of completion 2000
Location Singapore
Architect SCDA

Left Viewed from the street, the house reads as a series of layered planes of varied materials, textures and levels of opacity.

Right Behind the street wall, the layering develops in three dimensions: screen walls, projections and the flat entry canopy signify functional elements such as the front door, screened internal volumes and a trellis through to the garden behind.

The Coronation Road West House is an urbane townhouse built within a precinct of detached suburban houses. Sitting on a relatively small site, this family home is deceptively large. Taking advantage of a play of layered surface planes and contrasting materials – concrete, stone, timber and steel – the three level house is pushed as close as possible to the front rock-faced street wall, which itself becomes part of the overall composition. In effect, the house becomes a collage of elements that conceals its scale, and only hints at the transparency of the house's rear elevation, which overlooks a relatively large garden and generously-scaled swimming pool. The composition is also made more complex by the appearance from the street of a major and a minor 'house', each with floating flat parasol roofs, and each appearing to sit above an off-form reinforced concrete wall. The smaller of the two 'houses' is, however, a study pavilion cantilevering towards the street to the west, and sitting over the eastern swimming pool. The roof of this pavilion floats entirely free of the timber slatted box beneath; and a timber lattice screen, which infills a large cutout in the main concrete wall, throws a gridded shadow across the pool terrace. SCDA deploy skilful planar composition in the horizontal and vertical dimension: a tactic to denote the house's public face and an image of civility. It also becomes a way of creating privacy, a way of reducing scale and of providing shade.

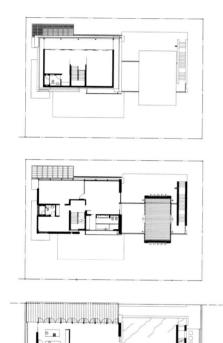

Level three

Level two

Level one

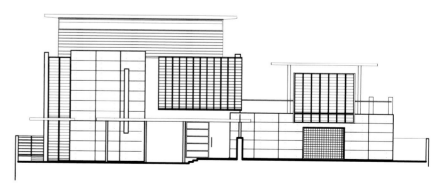

West elevation

Andrew Road House

Year of completion 2003
Location Singapore
Architect SCDA

A meditation on open and closed form, the Andrew Road House comprises three prismatic volumes laid out in a U-shape around a swimming pool, which functions as the linking piece in one of SCDA's most accomplished dialogues on formalist composition. The house is large, and the impression of scale is heightened by the courtyard arrangement of the three volumes. From the street, this complex dialogue is only hinted at, as the house is set well back within a spacious green lawn in a suburb of large and expensive houses. To the right, a timber-clad box leaps out from behind a solid fin wall, which is clad in stone veneered in a rich striated pattern. A flat parasol roof sits above the timber box, which contains bedrooms above and living spaces below. A thin parasol roof also floats above a second prismatic volume: a gracious, entirely open terrace/entry/sitting hall platform floating in a reflecting pool and overlooking the swimming pool. The effect is surprising, one expects to enter the house itself, but there is instead a sense of having been received into an open-sided pavilion fit for an outdoor regal reception. To one's left is the third prismatic volume, with another floating flat parasol roof above walls clad in a permeable metal screen, and where semi-transparency, shade and light at night create the effect of a diaphanous lantern. Around and between these three forms is a landscape of pools and floating stepping-stones. The whole compound creates the effect of dwelling within a three-dimensional architectural tapestry: one of inlay, embossing and layering with stone, steel, glass and water.

Left The reveals to the striations in the stone clad entry wall are deeper than those of the taller wall behind, casting shadows and heightening the effect of ground-hugging mass. The ceremonial reception area floats above shallow pools and thin concrete walkways in a calm and decorous spatial composition.

Left A lower pavilion can be seen from the reception area. Its gentle metallic appearance and Miesian proportions provide a textural counter-point to the monumental stonework of the taller pavilion across the pool.

Right The overall effect of the complex is as if the hovering Prairie Style roofs of Frank Lloyd Wright's Robie House (1905) have been fully embraced by the anti-gravitational aspirations of De Stijl. Such a description is not frivolous, but a key clue to the skill with which SCDA are able to manipulate form and materials.

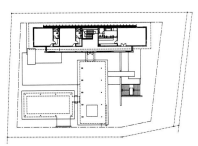

Level two

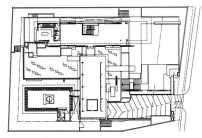

Level one

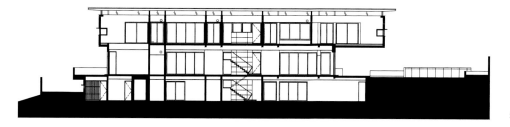

Section

Lincoln Modern

Year of completion 2003
Location Singapore
Architect SCDA

Left The graphic diagram of Lincoln Modern is one of two towers infilled with split level apartments. Separating the two is a flight of open-air escape stairs.

Opposite A lap pool and garden area on the eastern side of the apartment block. The aluminium curtain wall, orange fin walls and grey concrete of the tower provide an architectonic contrast to the exotica of the resort-like landscape.

Lincoln Modern is a 30-storey condominium tower, housing 56 split-level two and three-bedroom apartments, studios and penthouses. SCDA's design is an experiment in apartment typology: it is Singapore's first residential tower to feature six-metre tall loft-like living spaces in a unit with single level bedroom floors. Each apartment interlocks within the half-depth of the tower, and this can be read on the building's façade. The whole scheme can be seen as fitting a timber puzzle together within two vertical egg-crate forms, which was in fact how the building was constructed. Lincoln Modern is essentially a pair of concrete-framed towers, with the gaps between those towers filled with escape stairs, lifts and services. The result is a high-rise screen that recalls French architect Le Corbusier's unbuilt apartment and office tower proposals in Algiers and Rio de Janeiro, whose appearance was of a high-rise *brise soleil*: but there are two main differences. The first is that Lincoln Modern does not have apartments crossing over the full-dimension of the tower width, as achieved by Le Corbusier at his Unite d'Habitation, Marseilles (1948-53); instead at Lincoln Modern, there is a central corridor. The second difference is that the slim elegance of SCDA's glazed curtain wall, louvres and anodised aluminium cladding is given further graphic strength by two orange fins which slice up the centre of one façade, while one orange fin divides the composition of the other elevation into a Suprematist sculpture. At ground level, the eastern face of the building drops into a swimming pool with floating palm trees – heroic form terminates in resort comfort! At one level, Lincoln Modern is an important demonstration of the need in Singapore to creatively explore density in respect to new demographic types, and to use interior volume as a way of imparting variety to the spatial experience of high-rise living. At another level, this building demonstrates SCDA's ability to blend assured formalism with programmatic innovation.

Left A giant urn forms a visual marker at ground level on the western entry side of Lincoln Modern, forming a decorative element flanking a shallow pool. Adjustable louvres provide ventilation at each level of the lift lobby.

Opposite The street face of the building is a description of functional delineation, including louvred service zones and stairs. From below, it appears that one is looking upward at a Constructivist fantasy from the 1920s.

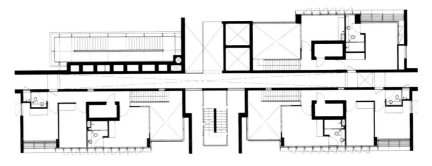

Upper floor plan

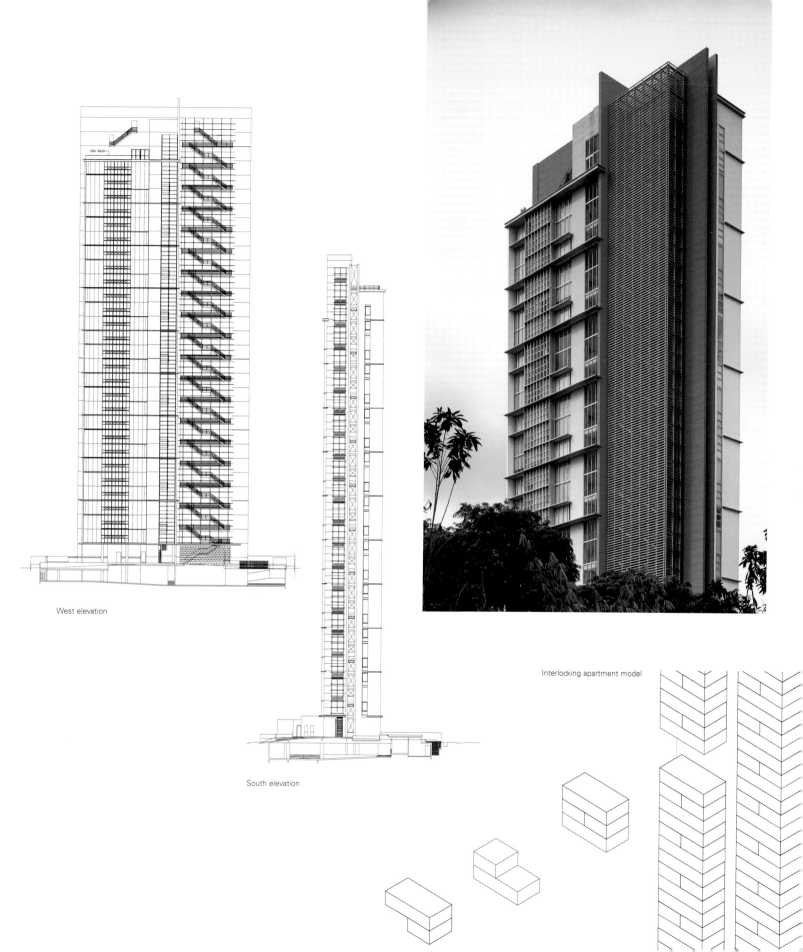

West elevation

South elevation

Interlocking apartment model

The Ladyhill

Year of completion 2002
Location Singapore
Architect SCDA

Located in an exclusive area near Orchard Road, the Ladyhill apartments have been built on the site of the former Ladyhill Hotel. The 55-unit condominium has been planned as two parallel strips of terrace-house-like apartments facing what is essentially a fully landscaped garden 'street': as if cars, footpaths, streetlights and the accretions of urban life have been removed in favour of a green 'street' garden, complete with mature 'street' trees. This 'street' culminates with a swimming pool and timber deck that cantilevers above a lower courtyard, gymnasium and basement carpark. Facing this accomplished piece of urban landscape by Tierra Design, the architects have delineated the 'public' face of the four-storey blocks as a series of layered screened elements – glass, stone and steel – capped by floating flat eaves: though with the reassuring forms of gable roofs when the blocks are seen end-on. This dexterous public screen along the length of the linear garden conceals deep cuts into the façade, and a series of lightwells are located deep in the centre of and along the length of each block. A typical terrace house or shophouse plan has been reconfigured, so that natural light is provided to all the major and minor rooms of every apartment, including kitchens and bathrooms. It is as if SCDA have carved form away from a typical slab block to provide the pragmatic requirements of light and ventilation. They have then reclad each block, concealing the designed 'erosion' of its form and providing an urbane filigree to the garden in front. The building itself appears to possess the equivalent of a tree's trunk, branches, twigs and leaves: a series of graduated elements which becomes an efficient mediator of climate, privacy, light and air.

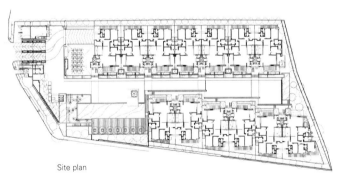

Site plan

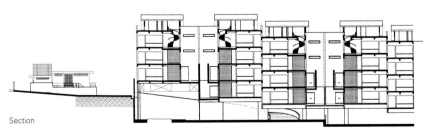

Section

Left The living room overlooks the swimming pool and terrace enclosed by the L-shaped volume. The internal stone wall of the entry hall becomes the external wall of the family/kitchen wing. The double height volume of the entry hall is graced by a chandelier of contemporary design.

Right From the garden, the house appears as a compositional exercise of formal opposites. Deep cutouts and recessed window walls at ground level have been used instead of eaves to provide shading.

The Dalvey Estate House is a comfortable two storey family home set deep on a sloping site in an affluent residential precinct. At its lowest point, the site is about five metres below the road level, and the architects took this as a challenge, designing the house as if it was a giant L-shaped retaining wall, transparent at ground level and solid on the first floor; embracing a swimming pool within the bend of the L-plan. It is a retaining wall that breathes, and makes clear the distinction between public and private realms. When landscaping matures, the house will discreetly recede from view. From the street, the distinguishing feature is a hovering black oblong form clad by spaced horizontal timbers, with a rectangular cutout modulated by adjustable vertical metal louvres, which have their leading edge perforated with tiny holes. This black form is a children's bedroom box floating above the main living room and study. By contrast, the master bedroom box sits above a dining room, kitchen and family room, but it is recessed from the stone-clad box below. With this house, SCDA move closer towards uncompromising abstraction, leaving behind obvious tropical signature elements: inverting the obvious modernist habits of abstraction. Instead of floating planes as climatic mediators to provide shade and to lighten the building form, SCDA use insulating thickness and deep cutouts into volumes as new ways of considering location. This house is thus a laboratory for mass, but a hollow, adjustable and penetrable mass. The message may be that the ideas demonstrated in this house could have application across a range of dwelling scales, from repetitive L-shaped courtyard houses to a typical speculative house. For the moment, though, it is an accomplished compositional backdrop for gracious suburban living.

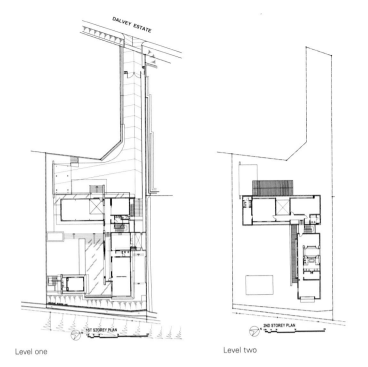

Level one

Level two

Above The stone-clad wall is striated: emphasising horizontality and direction-ality, and indicating the family/dining spaces a few steps below.

Right At night, the formal interplay of the volumes of the house reaches its climax as the light from within is reflected in the pool, and a doubling of the complex composition appears.

Right The timber clad upper level contains the children's bedrooms. A glass balustrade is virtually invisible, deferring to the deep cut-out of the volume.

Below A signature giant terracotta urn at the front door is recessed beneath the black bedroom box overhead. Fixed metal louvres appear as a bank of permanent 'gills', offering privacy and shielding the house from the western sun.

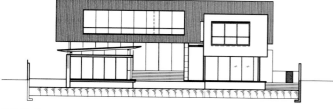

East elevation

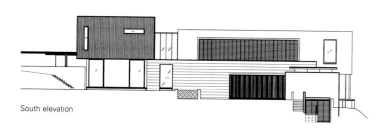

South elevation

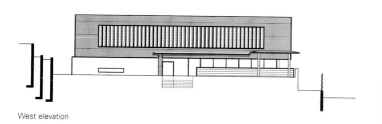

West elevation

Eko Prawoto

Eko Agus Prawoto (born Yogyakarta, Indonesia, 1959)
graduated in architecture from Gadjah Mada University,
Yogyakarta, Indonesia in 1982. He gained a Master of
Architecture degree from the Berlage Institute, Netherlands
in 1993, partly under the supervision of Balkrishna V Doshi.
Prawoto worked for PT Prima Design in Yogyakarta from
1980 to 1985, before establishing his own practice.
As Dean of the Faculty of Engineering at Duta Wacana
Christian University, Yogyakarta, Prawoto combines teaching
and architectural practice. His work has been exhibited in
Guangzhou, Helsinki, London, Matsidai, Niigata, Yogyakarta,
and also in Venice, where his installation, 'Housing for Urban
Poor' was featured at the 2000 Venice Architecture Biennale.
Important completed projects in Indonesia include the Gereja
Christian Church, Sokaraja, Central Java (1994-1995); Mella
Jaarsma & Nindityo House, Yogyakarta (1995); Cemeti Art
House, Yogyakarta (1997-1999); Butet Kertarajasa House,
Yogyakarta (2001-02); House for Ning, Yogyakarta (2002);
and the House for Jeannie and Lantip, Yogyakarta (2003-04).
His work has been published in *The Jakarta Post* and
Singapore Architect. Prawoto curated the exhibition of
the architecture of the late YB Mangunwijaya, the well-
respected Javanese priest, architect, writer and educator.

Essay and project descriptions by Amanda Achmadi

Eko Prawoto considers his works as ongoing architectural speculations on spatiality for living and about notions for living in Yogyakarta.

The work of Eko Prawoto in Yogyakarta exemplifies another face of modern architectural history in Indonesia, markedly different from that of Jakarta and Bali. His buildings speak of a more hybrid and fluctuating architectural culture than Jakarta's imagined metropolitanism and Bali's demanded authenticity. Yogyakarta, in Central Java, is home to the Keraton (palace and court) of the charismatic Hamengkubuwana monarch, and to Gajah Mada University, one of the oldest and largest universities in Indonesia. It is also home to an established intellectual tradition and to progressive contemporary art movements, within which Prawoto is a key participant. Yogyakarta has undergone dynamic historical unfolding, moulded by episodes of 'acculturations' between Hindu, Buddhist, and Islamic traditions, which have bequeathed a cultural fusion now known as Javanese culture. It has also been a site of colonial and postcolonial imaginings of Indonesian identity, and this flux of power struggles and progressive intellectual traditions has ensured the ongoing questioning of identity in Yogyakarta.

The city's urban history is marked by: the Keraton complex, which consists of a series of squares and palaces combining the Javanese aristocratic dwelling typology and the perceived idioms of European aristocratic style; colonial buildings exemplifying Tropical Dutch, Dutch Art Deco, Indies architecture and other colonial models for the Dutch East Indies; and the *limasan* pavilion of the kampung, with its bamboo woven enclosure and tilted pitched roof.

On the one hand, Prawoto is concerned with the degradation of Yogyakarta's kampung, and the disappearance of local timber and bamboo craftsmanship, such as the split double bamboo connection used in long-span roof construction. Most of his projects are situated in urban villages and suburban areas, and are thus directly engaged with the issue of urbanization. On the other hand, Prawoto embraces an innovative quest for modernity and a critical questioning of the modern capitalist identity embraced since Indonesia's independence. In articulating his contextual approach, Prawoto combines a climatic design strategy with an exploration of new formal possibilities and construction systems, based on local craftsmanship and vernacular building typologies. None of Prawoto's projects reproduce traditional dwelling forms: instead, he considers his works as ongoing architectural speculations on spatiality for living and about notions of contemporary Yogyakarta. These experiments include careful study of existing patterns of activity, so that new functions can be implanted as active cells within a larger context, and intimate transitions of scale and sequential dialogue can be created between any new structure and its surrounding typologies. The results are inspiring alternatives to the conservationist's 'museumization' of Yogyakarta's architectural traditions.

Prawoto detaches himself from the *pendapa*-ization of architecture in Java. This refers to the recent Javanese phenomenon whereby a *pendapa* structure (the veranda-space enclosed by a square-shaped pitched roof supported by grids of wood columns) is reproduced at almost every scale of building, without any degree of reinterpretation or appropriation. Contemporary scholars read this phenomenon as a legacy of Dutch architectural discourses on Java and of Suharto's "repressive traditionalism", as both these episodes of political perception of architectural identity selected *pendapa* as the main symbol of Java's architectural tradition. Prawoto rejects the elevation of this one architectural element as a singular representation of a complex architectural culture.

Beyond this, Prawoto endeavours to position his client (and himself) as the contemporary subject, as an active participant within Yogyakarta's perceived cultural traditions. Among his clients are an outspoken political commentator and theatre performer, a journalist who is the recipient of an Indonesian humanity award, a dancer, and installation artists and curators of contemporary art. His clients are also critical of the political value of the *pendapa*, seeing it as the property of the aristocrats or of the economically powerful. In the case of the Cemeti Art House (1997-99), the client insisted on the use of the *limasan* roof which, unlike the *pendapa*, epitomizes peasant traditions. For Cemeti art society, the *limasan* roof symbolizes their vision of an accessible art. The House (2002) for Maria Hartiningsih (a respected journalist and writer) exemplifies her critique of the commodification of modes of habitation in big cities in Java, including Yogyakarta. She refused to have a guest room unit, a typical product of modern housing estates, and instead, asked Prawoto to simplify the house programme, hence avoiding the symbolic reproduction of a speculative icon.

The significance of Eko Prawoto's works lies in their thoughtful impact on their clients' lives and contexts. His aesthetic lies beyond immediate materiality and visual impact, and he demonstrates the way space-making unfolds as a complex interaction between place, user and architecture. One might be overcome by the diverse textures resulting from combinations of materials, formal languages and compositions in Prawoto's work, and this blending could be read as an easy embrace of eclecticism, distracting from the rationale behind his architecture. But in contemporary Indonesian architectural discourse, Prawoto's experiments should be read as another form of resistance to the simplistic pictorial reproduction of the country's architectural traditions. While other architects articulate this resistance by succumbing to the modern 'other,' Prawoto's architecture suggests another possibility. It embodies his ambition of becoming a contemporary subject of his own architectural tradition, where modernity is conceived as a utopian spirit to be contextualized and claimed, while the material remarks of architectural tradition are considered as episodes of an unravelling history.

House for Jeannie and Lantip

Year of completion 2004
Location Yogyakarta, Indonesia
Architect Eko Prawoto

This house belongs to a young family: a pair of classical Javanese dancers and their baby. American-born Jeannie and Lantip, from Yogyakarta, continue to learn and explore both the skills and history of classical Javanese dance. Embodying the couple's progressive spirit, the house, within a kampung on the western outskirts of Yogyakarta, is designed as a hybrid structure combining a circular wall and a grid of columns on the ground floor, with *limasan* wooden pavilions on the upper floor. A sunken circular space below the ground floor contains a pantry-dining space and the dancing studio. This ground floor space is a contrast to the upper floor, which consists of contained bedroom and bathroom units nestled underneath a *limasan* roof. A continuous open balcony on the upper floor provides a viewing platform overlooking the adjacent kampung. Eko Prawoto explores a dialogue with the kampung's architecture by establishing a new, but carefully composed building typology. He invokes the possibility of a formal dialogue between the architecture and its context, by resisting a stereotypical and uncritical architectural interpretation of a place. By elevating an entire representation of the vernacular *limasan* house to the first floor, and by using slim concrete columns and beams to support it, Eko Prawoto has repeated his formula in which the 'local' building tradition is 'expanded' rather than simply reproduced. Jeannie and Lantip hold dancing classes at their house, and the circular wall on the ground floor was inspired by the circular movements in a classical dance repertoire. Here, Prawoto has exercised his own engagement with another facet of traditional culture of Yogyakarta, as beyond the mystified elegance of classical choreographies, Prawoto considers dance fundamentally as a space making activity.

Above The view from the balcony: a contemporary interpretation of a space intrinsic to indigenous, colonial and modern building forms across the tropical Asian region.

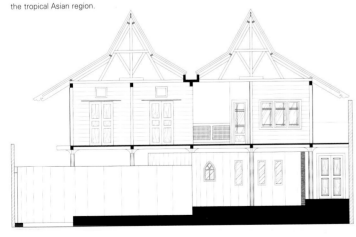

Section

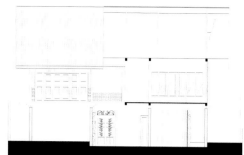

Section

Left Eko Prawoto is not averse to deploying traditional roof forms and formal imagery, but here he elevates these elements above a rationalist frame of concrete beams and columns.

Above The lofty sunken terrace, surrounded by gardens and a tall neighbouring wall, is a cool retreat that doubles as a dance studio and performance space.

Gereja Christian Church

Year of completion 1995
Location Sokaraja, Central Java, Indonesia
Architect Eko Prawoto

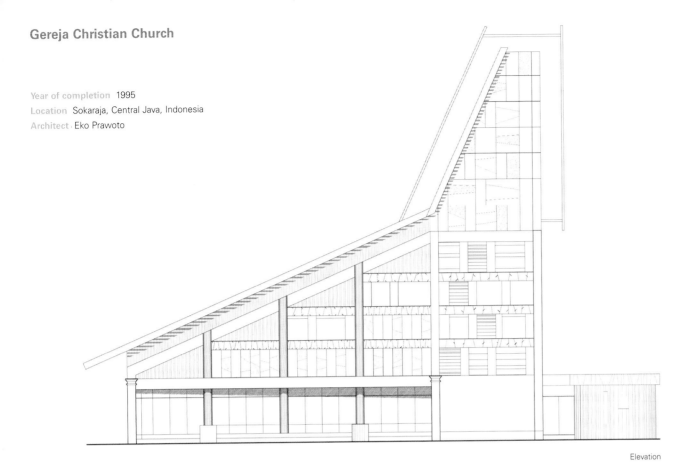

Elevation

The strong visual symmetry and towering structures of classical European church typology has been widely reproduced in Indonesia, but the Gereja Church in Sokaraja, a composition of mass and translucent surfaces, speaks of a humble asymmetric volume and a dextrous play of light. The building takes the shape of a volume divided and left open at its axis. In front of this halved volume is an open plaza, and the volume's front 'urban' face, where it appears to have been split from its other half, creates a stunning panoply of colour and transparency. The east-facing mosaic composition of stained-glass windows and sunshading partitions illuminates an internal space rich in textures, tones and shadows. The spatial hierarchy, orientation and verticality of a church's inner space is usually created through disciplined visual, layout and elevational symmetry, but Eko Prawoto achieves this by means of the subtle movement of the rays of light passing over the altar. Without succumbing to rigid and predictable symmetry, Prawoto has produced an appropriate and quietly unassuming monumentality.

Opposite The dynamic totemic profile of the Gereja Church reaches upward: a mysterious silhouette that evokes images of indigenous Javanese roof forms.

Above The eastern entry wall is a screen of stained glass, louvres and folding doors. As the roof rises, the ceiling transforms itself into a soaring and spectacular extrapolation of its structure.

House for Butet Kertarajasa

Year of completion 2002
Location Yogyakarta, Indonesia
Architect Eko Prawoto

Section

Butet Kertarajasa, a popular theatre performer, writer, and political commentator, asked Eko Prawoto to create a democratic home for his family with the ambience of a village. Situated in a suburban area in Yogyakarta, this task was combined with a requirement to revitalize an existing building, a typical low-cost residential unit. Prawoto responded to this task by building a number of pavilions around the site with a similar scale to the existing building, without being overly concerned with blending the old and new. Each pavilion contained a bedroom unit belonging to each member of the family, with the largest pavilion at the front containing outside and inside living areas, and a carport on the ground floor level. A number of courtyards and pathways were created as connectors in Kertarajasa's 'village', and this strategy achieves the spontaneous fluidity of the kampung, where one form blends with another, not because they are rigidly designed as one harmonious or united composition, but because each built element greets and never turns its back to the others. No singular and fixed perspective point can be found in the house, and each inhabitant embarks on their own discovery of the house. An open timber staircase was situated as the core of the site, and here a personal memento was poetically implanted. Originating from an old wooden rice grinder, each step of the staircase is a wooden plank with a hole in the middle: Eko Prawoto filled this whole with transparent acrylic and inserted old receipts of Kertarejasa's writing honorariums dated back to the late 1970s. Most of the doors and windows used in the house were recycled, collected from flea-markets and demolished old buildings in Central Java. Kertarejasa considers this house as his kampung, where no clear boundary exists between inside and outside.

Opposite The view over the dining room to the garden shows the eclectic array of crafted details which decorate the rational architectural frame.

Right Handcraft is to be seen everywhere, side by side with the reinforced concrete frame. Detail is inlaid into each stair tread, and every element celebrates the hand.

House for Mella and Nindityo

Year of completion 1995
Location Yogyakarta, Indonesia
Architect Eko Prawoto

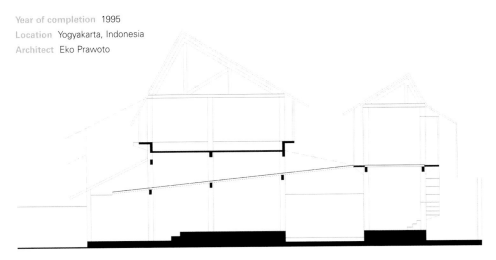

Section

Left A cylindrical volume painted in a bright neon yellow is a pivotal element in this house, and it creates a dynamic counterpoint within what is otherwise a long linear volume. Inside it is a small bathroom where, functioning as light and ventilation channels, three openings in the bathroom's circular wall were carved by Nindityo as a response to Prawoto's architectural composition.

Opposite Mella and Nindityo's House is a collector's gallery as much as a house, and could be seen as a museum of their autobiography: the house becomes a journey through their artistic meanderings.

This was Eko Prawoto's first project following his studies at the Berlage Institute, a period of time which gave him the opportunity to experience 'distance' from his 'local' Yogyakarta. Such distance was important for it allowed him to see and inquire, rather than being consumed by the familiar realm and identity of Yogyakarta. His clients, progressive installation artists and painters, Mella Jaarsma and Nindityo, are also individuals who constantly exercise a process of distancing themselves from the objective world and its surroundings. Jaarsma, a Dutch-born artist, and Nindityo, an Indonesian artist, have curated a series of contemporary art exhibitions known for their dense social criticism.

A central requirement was for the availability of space and surfaces to enclose and inspire creative activities, as well as to exhibit their collection of artworks. The clients also envisaged a room that might grow for their young daughter. Situated on a long and narrow site in the middle of a small kampung pocket in the middle of Yogyakarta, Prawoto positioned an open ramp corridor as the backbone of the house. This ramp ensures spatial connectivity between different zones of the house: the upper and the lower, and the front and the back. The ramp maximises the experience of the house's inner sanctum as a space to exhibit their collection of artworks, and at one point along the ramp, Prawoto provides a visual encounter between the family and their social and spatial contexts: the kampung. While the site is walled-in due to adjacent buildings, a daily journey across the ramp allows the family to greet their neighbours, as well as to see, hear, and sense the kampung. The ground floor consists of living, pantry, service areas, and a painting studio, while bedrooms and bathroom units are located on the upper floor. The careful arrangement of contained and open studio space in this narrow house, combined with the strategic positioning of the ramp, cylindrical volume and positioning of the artworks ensure the house's spatial fluidity. The result is rich and sequential unfolding of dynamic space.

Rahul Mehrotra

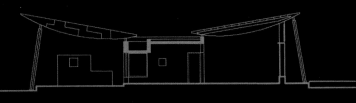

Essay and project descriptions by Philip Goad

Rahul Mehrotra (born New Delhi, India, 1959) graduated from
the School of Architecture, Ahmedabad in 1985 and as Master
of Architecture in Urban Design from Harvard University in
1987. From 1987 to 1988 he worked for Stull & Lee in Boston,
then in Bombay for Charles Correa from 1988 until 1990. In
1990 he established the office of Rahul Mehrotra Associates
in Bombay. Since 1994, he has been Executive Director of
the Urban Design Research Institute, Bombay and in 1995
he founded the conservation practice, The Bombay
Collaborative. He has taught at the National University of
Singapore (1998) and University of Michigan, Ann Arbor (2000,
2004) where is an Associate Professor. The firm's work has
been exhibited in Ankara, Berlin, London, Paris, Shanghai,
Tokyo and Vancouver. Important completed works include
the Shanti House, Alibag, India (1997); Film Maker's House,
Alibag, India (2001); the Laxmi Machine Works, Coimbatore,
India (1998); Cantonment Bungalow, Ahmedabad, India (2002);
Chowmahalla Palace restoration, Hyderabad (2002-); and the
Orchard House, Ahmedabad, India (2003). Mehrotra's work
has been published in numerous journals including *A+U*
(Japan), *Architectural Design* (UK), *Architectural Review* (UK),
Asian Architecture (Singapore), *Indian Architect & Builder*
(India) and *Monument* (Australia). Mehrotra was a contributor
to *World Architecture* 1900-2000, vol.8 (2000), and author
(with Sharada Dwivedi) of *Bombay – The Cities Within* (1995).

In the context of contemporary Indian architecture, the name Rahul Mehrotra is cited constantly, for many reasons. He possesses an impeccable pedigree: a graduate and Gold Medallist from one of India's top design institutions, the School of Architecture CEPT at Ahmedabad, and from the American Ivy League bastion, Harvard University; and work experience with Charles Correa, one of the great champions of regionalism for Indian architecture in the 1970s and 1980s. Beyond this, Mehrotra is a polymath for his profession: he is a gifted educator, writer, research and practice collaborator, film-maker, urbanist, heritage expert, scholar, and not least – an acclaimed architect. Often invited to be a keynote speaker, a juror on international design competitions and a conference panellist, Mehrotra speaks for Indian architecture and urbanism on the basis of a deep knowledge of its past. It is this interest in the history of the Indian city and its architecture, and the practice of heritage conservation, especially in Bombay (now known as Mumbai), which he describes as the archetypal 'Bazaar City' of South Asia, that underlies Mehrotra's approach to architectural design.

As architectural historian Jon Lang has observed, Mehrotra was, during the 1990s, not alone in his interests in historic preservation. Somaya & Kalappa in Mumbai, Jai Sen in Calcutta, Debashish Naik in Ahmedabad, Nalini Thakur in Delhi and Avanlika Chitnavis in Nagpur also immersed themselves in the historic Indian city and in a breadth of practice spanning adaptive re-use, restoration and empirical documentation. However, Mehrotra has distinguished himself from his compatriots with his ability to communicate these interests in verbal and written form, as well as through actual projects. His firm's restoration projects range from the vast scale and material richness of the Chowmahalla Palace (built from c.1750 onward) in Hyderabad (2002-) to the humble corrugated iron roof and basic form of an 1840s cantonment bungalow in Ahmedabad (2002). Critical career achievements for Mehrotra were his appointment in 1994 as Executive Director of the Urban Design Research Institute in Bombay and his founding of the conservation practice, The Bombay Collaborative, in 1995. Both these groups expanded the breadth and influence of architectural design within India's largest metropolis, now reckoned to have a population close to 20 million. These were strategic moves for Mehrotra. History could become a radical tool within a city poised on the brink of development and in a constant state of chaotic flux. Preservation became not just a way of understanding the city, but also a way of working positively with local authorities, and gauging and controlling the city's value in terms of public space, typology, morphology, monuments, and the labyrinthine grain of streets, alleys and bazaars. It was also a form of responsible resistance.

In Mehrotra's independent practice, the lessons gained from history and local material practice are invariably brought into elegant counterpoint with progressive technologies. Yet these architectural gestures are quiet and non-demonstrative. They highlight such fundamental elements as a wall, a window, steps and the frame. The Shanti Weekend House at Alibag (1997), across the water south of Bombay, employs local load-bearing masonry techniques combined with a technically sophisticated steel-framed skillion roof. Also at Alibag, the Film Maker's House (2001) has similarly heavy massed walls faced in local stone, which shelter dark mysterious interiors with deep reveals to small window openings. The dark coolness of the interior contrasts strongly with the external fly-away roofs propped off spindly steel columns. Heavy and light, dark and light become simple but effective design themes that resonate with the spareness of the surrounding landscape. The Orchard House (2003) at Ahmedabad is a starkly beautiful house, which does not deliberately echo the sculptural exuberance of Le Corbusier's renowned work in Ahmedabad, such as the Sarabhai House (1955) or the Shodhan House (1956). Mehrotra appears to draw more lessons from the muted subtle massing and saturated colours of Mexican master, Luis Barragan. In this spacious courtyard house, water becomes the contrasting element of lightness and coolness against the massive surrounding walls that bake and radiate colour in the blazing heat of Ahmedabad.

Mehotra's architecture in these detached residential projects reveals his fondness for aesthetic restraint in design. Yet he is not averse to including such conventional architectural elements as the all-encompassing roofs seen in his factory for STP Construction Additives, Goa (1995) and in the corporate headquarters building for Laxmi Machine Works Group at Coimbatore (1996-98), where huge gabled roofs provide cooling shade and large amounts of covered space without the need for air-conditioning. The symbolic value as well as the practical function of the roof is, for Mehrotra, not an element to be feared or avoided. Too often a roof with a pitch or a hip is disregarded for its obvious semiotic value, as if its use might attract a 'regionalist' label of genuflection towards a colonial past, or be seen as weakness on the part of the architect's aesthetic resolve. The bias towards abstraction holds only limited value for Mehrotra, and he scoffs at such preciousness. This is his strength as an architect. His work demonstrates comfort with working in valid modes, which depend on the specifics of each situation. Rahul Mehrotra cites a straightforward but essential mantra for tropical architecture: "buildings that breathe, that make places in the shade…"

Shanti House

Year of completion 1997
Location Alibag, Maharashtra, India
Architect Rahul Mehrotra

Below The curve of the living room ceiling follows the curve of the roof as it emerges on the outside of this courtyard house. Here the cool shade of the living room is a retreat from the heat of the day.

Located across the harbour from Bombay in the rural landscape of Alibag with its softly rounded hills and spreading farms, this weekend house designed for an urban couple is an exercise in combining two regional archetypes; the courtyard and the verandah, but in an updated architectural form. Designed to sit as blocks between two parallel walls of load-bearing masonry, the house comprises two open-ended courts with contemporary versions of the verandah facing the garden landscapes: a third courtyard forms the house's centre and entry court. The external walls are faced in natural stone with a single central cutout opening, and these walls seem to stretch endlessly into the semi-rural landscape. In the central court, the walls are plastered over and painted a dusky pink, with white painted reveals showing wall cutouts and timber *jalis* inserted into wall openings. A giant cutout in the courtyard walls provides a view through to an open living room, and beyond to a verandah terrace. There, the verandah roof, framed in steel and with a slim skillion roof floating over the top, flies upward instead of down. He provides the house with a new type of sustainable feathered edge, a completely open living room flanked by enclosed rooms: suggesting lightness and lofty volume, rather than the mass and enclosure of the central courtyard.

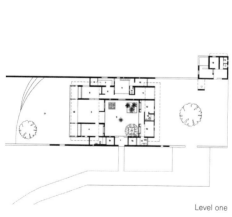

Section

Level one

Laxmi Machine Works
Corporate Headquarters

Year of completion 1998
Location Coimbatore, Tamil Nadu, India
Architect Rahul Mehrotra

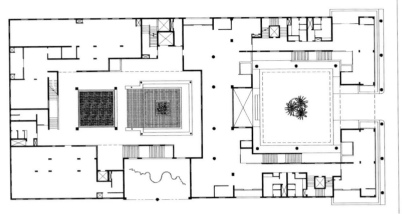

Level one

The corporate headquarters for the Laxmi Machine Works (LMW) in Coimbatore, southern India, houses the firm's eight subsidiaries within the one complex. The site of the office building with its three courtyards, each of a different size, is sandwiched between industrial establishments on one side and an army cantonment on the other. The three level building has a reinforced-concrete post and beam system with a series of hipped roofs framed in steel and clad in clay tiles. Instead of the common corporate image of a glazed office building, the LMW offices suggest a different recipe for the creation of Indian corporate identity: the forms of the building echo past building traditions, despite their sophisticated structural materials; and the inclusion of large bodies of circulating water in two of the courtyards provide both a psychological and climatic cooling effect. Internal circulation between enclosed offices is around these courtyards, along broad open corridors beneath the deep shade of the building's giant verandah roofs. An important component of the building's character is provided by the corporation's enlightened approach to filling the building with works of local crafts and contemporary art pieces. One such example draws directly from the LMW steel plant, where Indian designer Rajeev Seth collaborated with contemporary Indian artist Yogesh Rawal in executing metal *jalis* (perforated screens) made from scrap metal salvaged from the firm's plant. Throughout this building, Rahul Mehrotra has provided robust architectural bones, a clear framework that relies on direct climatic and material response, an approach that is simple rather than overstated.

Below Rahul Mehrotra encouraged artists to collaborate with him on the project, producing new versions of the *jali*, or terraced screen, by using as-found steel plate recycled from the Laxmi Machine Works steel plant. This screen wall is a collaboration between designer Rajeev Seth and Indian artist Yogesh Rawal.

Section

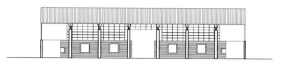

South elevation

Above The central 'cooling' courtyard of the office headquarters. Continuously circulating water flows down a spillway into the pool below, and the great sloping roofs become collecting devices for rainwater.

Left Contemporary works of Indian art combine with Rahul Mehrotra's robust framework to provide a uniquely local brand of corporate identity.

Film Maker's House

Year of completion 2001
Location Alibag, Maharashtra, India
Architect Rahul Mehrotra

Below The picturesque western garden face of this weekend retreat is formed by projecting rooms, which angle away from the main circulation spine, and are capped with fly-away roofs.

Opposite The only projection along the eastern rock wall is an open sided living terrace, shaded by a fly-away roof. Fixed panels of timber louvres are complemented by roll-down blinds.

An external exercise in stone walls and fly-away roofs, Rahul Mehrotra's design for a weekend house for a film-maker is also an exploration in the mystery and dark spaces of the passage. Instead of the courtyards contained between parallel walls of the nearby Shanti House (1997) built 4 years earlier, Mehrotra here compresses this dimension to create an internal street of visual surprise. One side of the passage, which forms the circulation spine of the house, is a long straight wall with cutouts to a dry landscape of tall spindly trees. On the other side of this passage is a series of angled walls enclosing rooms, and these walls read as different forms along a street, as if creating an urban landscape of buildings. Mehrotra has created his own internal film-set – an urban alleyway with pools of light casting almost night-time ambience from the circular skylights cut into the concrete roof. A verandah roof flies upward from the long straight eastern wall, and is propped off steel blade columns with timber louvre panel infills. The softly curved underbelly of this roof shades an outdoor living terrace. On the other side of the house, two fly-away roofs demarcate the enclosed forms that are experienced along the internal corridor. To complete the sense of theatre, one can climb a series of steps to a roof terrace between the low points of the opposing butterfly-like roofs. Mehrotra has pared architecture to its essentials – wall, roof, enclosure, and semi-enclosure. There is, in this landscape, little need for anything else. There is mystery in the dark, there is release and repose in the light.

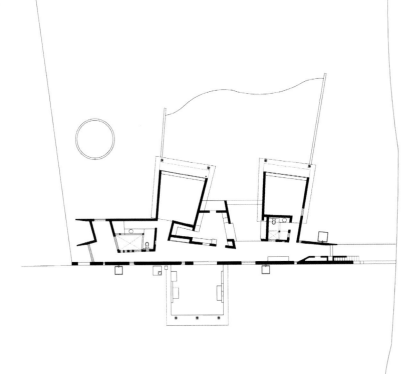

Right Looking along the rock-face wall to the semi-enclosed terrace. The curved underbelly of the verandah roof appears like the draped curve of a canvas shade.

Opposite A view from the northern entry along the major circulation space, the cool dark spine of the house. An array of surfaces and elements provide differing qualities of light: a highly reflective polished concrete floor; a white wall; reveals in red and yellow; and a circular skylight, which drops a pool of light from above.

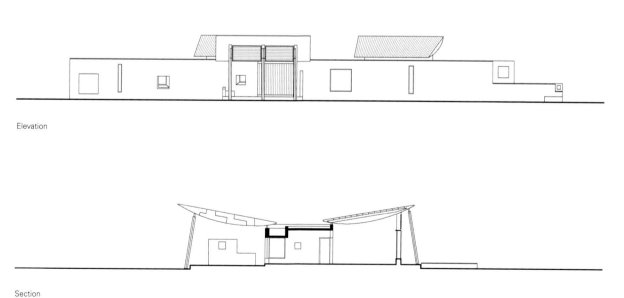

Elevation

Section

Below At the northern entry
end of the spine wall, a set
of steps leads to a roof
terrace where one can enjoy
the cool of the evening.

Right The emphasis on mass
is accentuated by the cutting
of small openings into the
long western wall. The highly
polished floor becomes the
major light source of this
cool 'urban passage'.

Cantonment Bungalow

Year of completion 2002
Location Ahmedabad, Gujarat, India
Architect Rahul Mehrotra

Below Seen across the lawn in the cool of the evening, the soft internal lighting emphasises the bungalow's all-encompassing hip roof and its perimeter colonnade of white washed brick piers.

Opposite In addition to the restoration work, large lily ponds were constructed adjacent to the house for cooling as well as aesthetic purposes.

Section

Much of Rahul Mehrotra's practice involves the conservation of historic buildings. The subtle alterations, additions and modifications that are invariably necessary in the adaptive reuse of such structures are a much under-discussed aspect of heritage work, anywhere in the world. Sensitively transforming an historic building so that contemporary use and heritage significance can be equally satisfied, requires consummate skill and control. It is a demanding discipline. Mehrotra was commissioned to restore an 1840s house in the Ahmedabad Cantonment: an early example of colonial bungalow architecture, a house set within a one-acre compound densely planted with trees. Constructed of brick with lime-plastered walls, timber rafters and corrugated iron roof, the bungalow has a deep encircling verandah with a double row of vertical supports: the outer colonnade consists of square brick piers, while the inner colonnade is a series of serenely proportioned Tuscan Doric columns. One of Mehrotra's tasks was to restore this extremely elegant double peripteral colonnade, as well as widening a section of the existing raised verandah floor, installing new plumbing and wiring, and creating a dining space. Another task was to introduce large water bodies – lily ponds – close to the bungalow as decorative cooling mechanisms. While these were contemporary interventions, the replastering and strengthening of the structure was carried out using traditional materials such as lime plaster, a black cement floor, and recycled timbers. A key concept was not to lose the ambience and humble grandeur of the original bungalow: authenticity was not to be outdone by contemporary comfort. The result is a credit to Mehrotra's masterful balance between old and new.

Above The extraordinary depth of the colonial bungalow's verandah was an extremely effective technique of countering the heat and providing gradations of living space, either closer or further from the light.

Left The restored sitting room, with painted and white washed walls and black concrete floors.

Opposite The double colonnade and outer perimeter of white washed brick piers, and an inner line of elegant Tuscan Doric columns give signs of a colonial pedigree. An extended floor at the end of the verandah has created a new dining space.

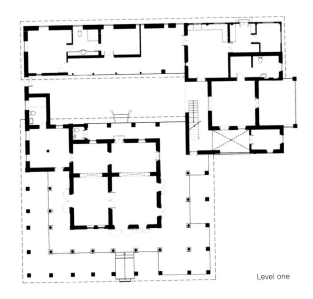

Level one

Above The service court has been refurbished as a landscaped garden with a lily pond and frangipani. Bamboo blinds supplement the already deep timber-framed verandah.

Right Internally, black concrete floors and yellow and white washed walls are the materials of the spare and simple, yet elegant interior. Even changes in floor level, with long deep treads, are techniques to slow movement in the heat.

Above The completed
bungalow, restored and
adapted for contemporary
living, remains one of the
most universally accepted
forms of living appropriate
to the tropics.

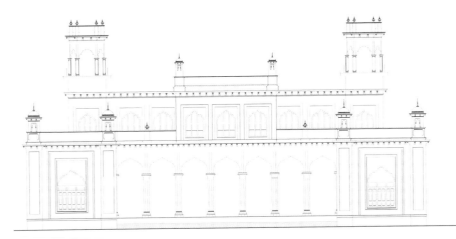

Khilwat Palace – elevation

Above left The exotic ceremonial interiors of the Khilwat Palace are being painstakingly restored, and the Nizam's throne room will be used as a museum. The Chowmahalla restoration project has been directed by the need to establish new and compatible uses for a magnificent ensemble of 18th Century architecture.

Above Many local craftsmen have worked on the restoration of the external and internal decoration of the complex. A sprawling collection of historic palaces and courtyards is being is being revitalized as an integral precinct within the multi-layered urban fabric of Hyderabad.

Khilwat Palace Restoration, Chowmahalla Palace

Year of commencement 2002
Location Hyderabad, Andhra Pradesh, India
Architect Rahul Mehrotra

One of Rahul Mehrotra's largest and most challenging restoration works has been the progressive restoration of the Chowmahalla Palace, Hyderabad, a lavish neo-Classical complex built by Nizam Salabat Jung in the 1750s. The palace, which comprises buildings laid out around two main courtyards, grew in incremental stages over the decades and with various changes in architectural style. The centrepiece building, the Khilwat Palace, contains the Darbar Hall (Throne Room), and it is being restored and converted into a museum to house costumes and artefacts from the Nizam's collection. The flanking rooms, which face into the courtyard and its water pools, were once guestrooms and have been adapted to serve as spaces for craftsmen to work in and sell their wares. The second half of the complex contains four palaces, also organised around a courtyard and water body, and these are to be restored to become museums explaining the Nizam's dynasty. Stage I of the project began in 2000 with detailed mapping, a fabric survey and the preparation of conservation reports for both restoration and adaptive reuse. Stage II involved stabilising the buildings under threat of collapse and carrying out emergency repairs. Stage III – the actual restoration – commenced in 2002, and includes the introduction of amenities to facilitate the general reuse of the structures. In all of this, Mehrotra has been at great pains to make any signs of new work recessive, and secondary to the important task of restoration. As with any such work, his architectural insertions clearly demarcate themselves from the original, never mimicking but taking a responsibly neutral position – in effect, the same position that he takes to his new buildings, where the integrity of a place, be it natural or built, is allowed to come forth. Like an artful diplomat, Rahul Mehrotra facilitates the elemental framework for that process to occur.

Above The colonnaded pavilions flanking the forecourt of the Khilwat Palace were stabilized and repaired, to be used as a centre for traditional arts and crafts in Hyderabad. The buildings surrounding the courtyard at the other end of the complex are being restored for use as an artist's retreat.

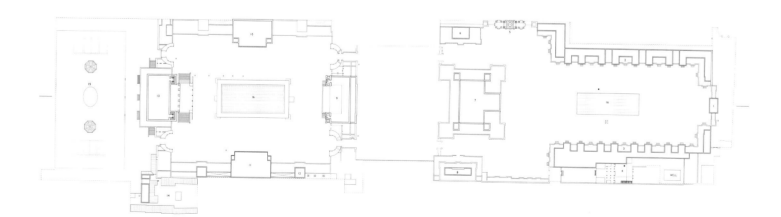

Site plan

Orchard House

Year of completion 2003
Location Ahmedabad, Gujarat, India
Architect Rahul Mehrotra

Below The polished concrete floor of the main living room complements the reflecting pool and its glassy stillness.

Opposite The blue pool, the blue wall, the polished floor and sheet glass combine to create an almost liquid cool interior.

Located five kilometres north of Ahmedabad in the centre of a eight hectare mango orchard, this low-slung single family weekend retreat is constructed of local Porbunder sandstone. In the midst of the leafy orchard, an open-side concrete rooftop pavilion is the only vertical feature of an earthbound house which emphasises the golden colours and textures of the semi-desert landscape. In Ahmedabad's hot dry climate, the orchard provides natural insulation for the house, and its shade and green leaves provide visual relief in the summer months when the glare is acute and uncomfortable. The rooms of the house are organized around a courtyard, which is the house's visual focus. The walls of the courtyard are painted brilliant white, the lap pool is tiled in blue, and one of the pool's blue walls emerges from the water and makes its way inside as a vertical wall; as does the pool as a flat reflective sculptural element in the living room. A framed opening in one of the white courtyard walls leads to a blank bright red wall, and outdoor concrete stairs lead upward from the courtyard to the concrete rooftop pavilion. From the gravelled entry court to the house's threshold beneath an archetypal concrete portal, the overall effect is that of arriving at an oasis: the entire sequence has been orchestrated as a procession towards an oasis of colour and of temperature. The final retreat is in the cool dark of evening, when one ascends to the rooftop terrace to catch any zephyr of breeze and to gaze across an horizon of mango treetops.

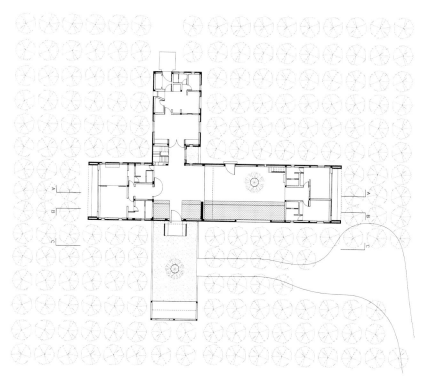

Level one

Below The gravelled eastern entry courtyard with a free-standing concrete entry portal and roof top belvedere. The external facing of the house is clad in the local Porbunder sandstone.

Opposite The courtyard, the walls and the lap pool take on an more ethereal yet limpid quality by night, enhanced by the brilliant red of a deep set wall and the pool lights.

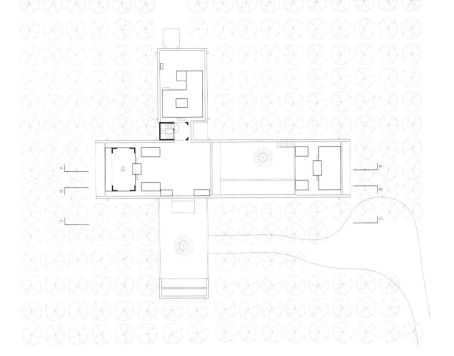

Level two

Above The black floor, a red wall, a blue wall, a white wall, bamboo blinds and heavy set furniture create a muscular De Stijl setting: one emphatically material rather than abstract, real rather than ideal.

Opposite The central courtyard, a serenely spartan place in the heat of the day, to be viewed from the shade within the house: a convincing expression of contemporary Indian minimalism.

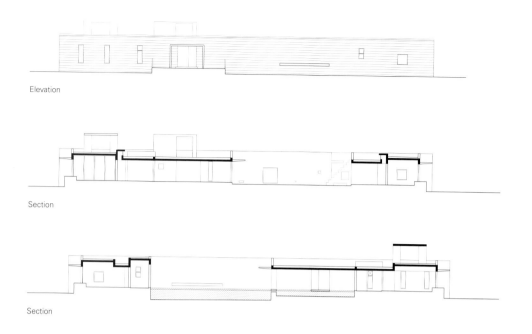

Elevation

Section

Section

W Architects

Mok Wei Wei (born Singapore, 1956) graduated from the National University of Singapore in 1982 and emerged as an architect under the mentorship of Singapore architect William Lim. From the early 1990s, he practiced in partnership within Lim's WLA architects, and then practiced as W Architects from 2003. Early work for Lim's practice explored Postmodern and Deconstructivist ideas, exemplified by the Church Cinema (1987); and the Tampines North Community Centre (1989). Mok Wei Wei has taught at the National University of Singapore and his work was exhibited at the Venice Biennale (2004). Important completed projects in Singapore include the Lem House (1995); the Morley Road House (1996); the Paterson Edge Apartments (1999); the Loft Condominium, Nassim Hill (1996-2002); Da Paolo e Judie Restaurant, Neil Road (2002); and the Arris Apartments, Yan Kit Road (1998-2003). His work has been published in *581 Architects of the World* (Japan), *Architectural Design* (Great Britain), *Architectural Review* (Great Britain), *Architectural Review Australia* (Australia), *Monument* (Australia) and *Singapore Architect* (Singapore).

Essay and project descriptions by Anoma Pieris

In his final design thesis at the National University of Singapore in 1982, Mok Wei Wei explored an intimate sensual experience organized around a cluster of buildings inserted into a constricted site in Singapore's Chinese heritage district. Situated within a shophouse perimeter, his project played with the changing scales and controlled vistas characteristic of a Chinese garden. In the post-recession period at the end of the 1980s, when Singaporean architects had the opportunity and time to develop more personal agendas, this early exploration provided important insight into a nagging personal question. Mok had tired of the constant search for stylistic representations and as he grew more reflective, chose to re-evaluate the familiar contradiction between formal articulation and subjective experience across various cultures. His father, who had been chief editor of a Chinese newspaper in Singapore until the mid 1980s, had introduced Mok to the Chinese literary tradition and it was to this inheritance that Mok now turned. As a Singaporean, educated in a Chinese-language school in an English speaking post-colony, and brought up with Chinese cultural values, Mok has begun to look for more personal sources of design inspiration.

The gardens in the Chinese city of Suzhou are one of the many tropes referred to by Mok in his analysis of subjective experiences. The representative qualities of landscapes are made familiar to us through Chinese landscape painting, especially the contrast between the 'Monumental' and 'Lyrical' styles that mark the beginning and ending of the Sung dynasty (960-1279). The contrast between the soaring mountains of the northern tradition and the more intimate and nostalgic landscapes of the southern, describe the inherent tensions that underpin artistic perceptions of space. Mok has translated these into architecture. In the Loft Condominium project (1996-2002) on Nassim Hill, these contrasts are played out in a language of granite walls, azure pools and drooping willow trees. Yet at the same time the landscape is asymmetrical, viewed obliquely in a denial of the familiar picturesque tradition. This conscious move away from tropical regional agendas to an East Asian source and to a diasporic interpretation of a warmer southern climate has taken Mok Wei Wei on an independent path of exploration. His main objective is to resolve the disjunction between a purely formal and a purely spatial approach, and to design for the specifics of place and collective history without becoming sentimental.

Mok's approach of designing a strong formal envelope which dissolves into a complex spatial experience is repeated in several recent designs. Where space is constrained in multi-storey projects such as the Paterson Edge (1999) or the Arris (1998-2003), the envelope is a glass curtain wall made impermeable by its reflection of foliage across the street. In Da Paolo e Judie (2002), a restaurant in a shophouse shell, the psychological experience of the interior becomes the subject of exploration. Mok inverts perceptions of hard and soft boundaries by fragmenting the interior of buildings, using hard materials to build a site's soft interior edge. In multi-storey projects, he treats a design as if it were a vertical landscape. Mok attributes the rhythm of these contrasts and the manipulation of spatial experience to another artistic medium introduced to him by his father: the classical novel in the tradition of the Chinese scholar/literati. Its most important example is The Story of the Stone or The Dream of the Red Chamber, a novel of manners of the feudal society which was brought down by the Cultural Revolution. In the novel, which recreates a romantic, melancholic imaginary, one gains intimate insights into the politics of family life, patronage, and the bureaucracy and social geography of the Ch'ing Empire (1644-1911). Mok finds the sensual intensity of the material world described in the novel inspirational. For example the following excerpt is a wonderful expression of movement through a Chinese garden:

…They had to walk round a stand of double-flowering ornamental peach trees and through a circular opening in a flower-covered bamboo trellis. This brought them in sight of the building's whitewashed enclosing wall and the contrasting green of the weeping willows which surrounded it…[…]…He led them inside the building. Its interior turned out to be all corridors and alcoves and galleries, so that properly speaking it could hardly have been said to have rooms at all. The partition walls, which made these divisions, were of wooden panelling exquisitely carved…

Mok's renewed interest in his Chinese heritage comes from a rejection both of Western stylistic agendas and of sentimental Orientalist constructions of tradition. His interest is in inserting vernacular sensibilities in terms of language and imagination back into the cache of valid cultural forms. The southern landscape in Chinese art and literature is closely related to his native Singapore, not only in a phenomenological sense but also in its cultural meanings. One sees this translation across geography in the Morley Road House (1996), where framing, layering and spatial compression recur around a loose configuration of pavilions. Oblique views of the pool and greenery recapture the episodic nature of the Chinese garden, without resorting to its iconic formal elements. Such translations of tradition into modernity are bold in an architect who is young and relatively removed from these cultural sources. Yet it is exactly this separation from the troubled history of modern China that gives diasporic architects such as Mok Wei Wei the freedom to interpret culture.

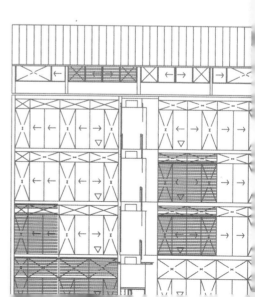

Morley Road House

Year of completion 1996
Location Singapore
Architect W Architects

The Morley Road House is Mok Wei Wei's most direct exploration of the intricacies of the Chinese garden and its spatial manouevres. Entered through a constricted opening off a public road, the house is designed as an orthogonal frame placed around six sequential zones. These separate zones, often contiguous and overlapping, constitute the many layers of experience within the site. One enters through a tightly compressed space into a loose configuration of pavilions organized by a series of stone walls.

With this house, Mok returns to his thesis project at National University of Singapore to deliberately reconstruct the experience of a bounded site, an oblique entry and a structured sequence of movement across a series of thresholds. From the legendary gardens of Suzhou, he takes the controlled sensuality of the fragmented experience, which is disclosed incrementally and edited as one passes through it to the next sequence. The intriguing dimension in this spatial unfolding is its narrative capacity, and its openness to multiple interpretations based on changes in light, volume, angle of vision and subjective position. In the hands of a sensitive designer, the experience is further abstracted into a Modernist template of external grey granite walls, which intersect with internal white planar surfaces, off-white marble floors and large expanses of glazing. An indoor pool mediates between soft and hard environments, with a cold reflective surface creating a sense of expansiveness.

Flat concrete roofs supported on slender concrete columns cantilever beyond the walls, and abstraction carries the spatial expressions far from their historic corollary of heavily detailed baroque interiors into a lighter world of pure sensations.

Opposite A monumental terrace and roof extend out across a reflecting pool. This full panorama of a house across water recalls the aristocratic villas of Suzhou.

Above A series of stone fin walls extends into the garden: the western approaches to the house are fragmented into a series of framed views.

Above The internal spaces are minimal formalist compositions of precious materials and skylit whiteness.

Opposite Seen across the garden, the roof above the terrace repeats the theme of a heavily abstracted Chinese roof profile, supported on reinforced concrete columns rather than timber posts: a Modernist reading of the Chinese villa.

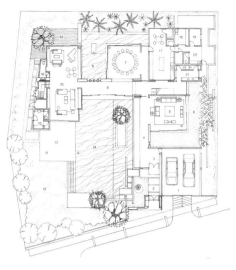

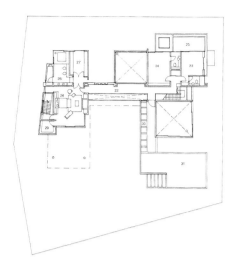

Level one

Level two

The Paterson Edge

Year of completion 1999
Location Paterson Road, Singapore
Architect W Architects

Level one

Situated on Paterson Road, adjacent to Singapore's busy Orchard Road commercial strip, the ten-storey apartment development was a surprising solution to a multi-storey residential brief. In a culture where apartments are typically imagined as functionalist concrete blocks or introverted high-rise condominiums, the idea of exposing the building through a glass curtain wall seemed unconscionable. Yet the glass wall is a conundrum in itself, raised above street level and acting as a boundary that clearly demarcates the edge of public territory. The façade of the long and narrow apartment building is protected by two environmental filters which veil the building's interior: the magnificent trees that flank Paterson Road and which are reflected on its surface; and the horizontal louvres that cast dappled light on the glazed façade. The building's palette of details has the clean lines of a steel and glass industrial aesthetic, and this differentiates it from the previous examples of Modernism replete in Singapore's landscape. It expresses neither the weight of the concrete frame, nor its functionalist agenda, merging instead into the context of elegant commercial complexes nearby. The Paterson Edge is a reflection of this context, rather than a statement on apartment life, and in doing so, poses a challenge regarding the negotiation of private life and public engagement in the life of the city.

Opposite The foliage of the trees becomes the inspiration for the curtain wall façade: variegated light reflections and changing patterns of shade, with the overall effect of reducing the heat of the sun.

Right Seen from the footpath, the eastern Paterson Road façade disappears into a repetitive veil of glazed sunshades.

The Arris Apartments

Year of completion 2003
Location Yan Kit Road, Singapore
Architect W Architects

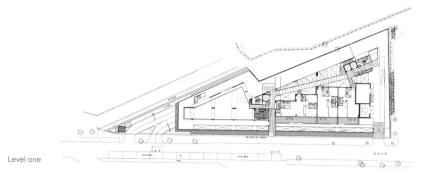

Level one

Designed after Paterson Edge and with a similar architectural vocabulary, the grouping of the Arris Apartments diverges from the purity of the Modernist master plan to explore the interior geography of the urban site. Located on an irregular shaped block of land with a tree-lined street front, Mok Wei Wei adopted the language of the glazed façade to build a boundary to the site. Reflecting the tall elegant roadside trees, the glazing presents a brittle yet impenetrable surface. The entryway is a discreet passage that leads through the building to its rear, and behind its glass façade, the building becomes an amorphous form. It changes its shape to satisfy variations in the brief, rising incrementally from seven to ten storey blocks with a solid wall wrapping it against the harsh western sun. A pool on the tenth floor perches precariously at the building's edge, giving views to the soaring cityscape beyond. The play of forms, sharp angles and oblique views along the rear façade creates a modulated spatial experience imperceptible from the street-front.

Opposite The startlingly thin profile of The Arris, seen from its southern end. The tapered form of the apartment slab and its attached sunshades read as a high rise glazed-in verandah.

Right The projections of the apartment building on the eastern façade accentuate its linear forms.

Da Paolo e Judie Restaurant

Year of completion 2002
Location Neil Road, Singapore
Architect W Architects

Below Second floor view: in contrast to Mok Wei Wei's use of glass and transparency in his apartment designs, the Paolo e Judie interior utilizes darkness and experimenting with light to create mood, mystery and subtle glamour.

Opposite Ground floor view: light from below, from slots in the walls and from the original shophouse light-well in the distance increase the sense of theatre.

Singapore's heritage agenda took firm shape during the late 1980s recession, when the Urban Redevelopment Authority established guidelines for the adaptive reuse of shophouse environments. Renovation almost always includes the conservation of the building façade, and the introduction of light wells and clerestory lighting to illuminate the deep plan of the shophouse. With the Da Paolo e Judie project, Mok Wei Wei responds to this programme with an unusual design solution: inserting a timber sleeve into the shophouse interior, creating a dark constricted space with glaring light at its two extremities. The restaurant is entered through a large door, which opens up the entire front of the shophouse to the street, and the effect of moving from light to dark effectively captures the sensations of the original shophouse. In Mok's architecture, one senses the associations that cling to the experience of place recreated ingeniously through the phenomenological perception of a familiar typology. Despite its minimalist vocabulary and modernist geometries, this project demonstrates that new work within an historic context can make a psychological link to the past.

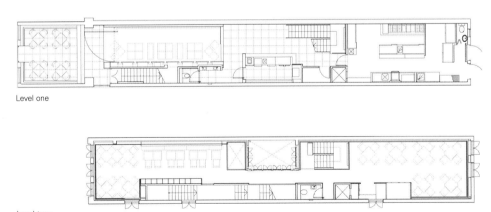

Level one

Level two

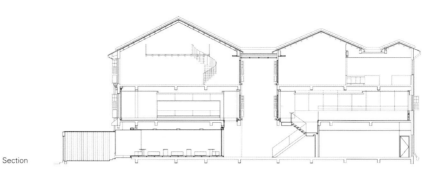
Section

The Loft Condominium

Year of completion 2002
Location Nassim Hill, Singapore
Architect W Architects

Using the perimeter block model as a solution to a low-rise apartment complex, Mok Wei Wei developed an historic site on Nassim Hill into a pleasant introverted environment. The design is for five separate blocks of four storeys (plus attic) each numbering seventy-seven units in total. The outer surfaces of the blocks are solid, forming a tight constraining boundary which conceals the private spaces of the apartments within. By contrast, the public living areas turn inwards towards a central communal courtyard. Materials are unapologetically Modern: white painted plastered walls, black powder-coated steel framed windows, steel and glass balustrades and stainless steel *brise-soleils*.

Following his interest in modeling space rather than form, in the manner of the Chinese gardens at Suzhou, Mok has designed a series of spatial essays in the landscape, positioning buildings strategically to frame views in and out of the site, and to preserve five century-old Tembusu trees. This spatial manipulation produces an asymmetrical geometry: the buildings appear to be yet another device in the landscape and part of its natural choreography. Stainless steel frames running vertically along the building's façade are

covered in vines, which draw the building further into the landscape.

The play of vertical and horizontal planes, where the ground moves upward along the surface of the wall or vines creep along steel frames on the building surface, invert the viewer's sense of gravity and sculp the surface of the site into a mountain landscape. A wall cuts diagonally through the site with a striated granite pattern interrupted by patches of Kyoto dwarf grass planted on the vertical surface: a humorous gesture by landscape designer Martin Polleros.

The mood within the complex is soft and ethereal: the drooping lines of willow trees, iridescent light reflected off a dark green lap pool and the subtle shifts of the many angular views across interlocking platforms recreates the quality of a monumental landscape experienced at a very intimate scale. Mok works against the colonial legacy of a luscious tropical 'picturesque' ideal to produce a more muted and moody space of introspection.

Elevation

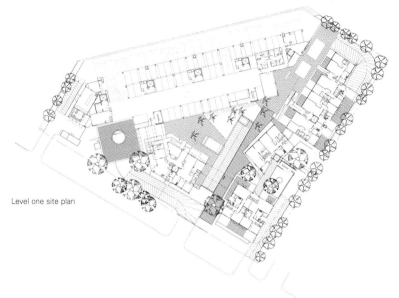

Level one site plan

Left The use of water and planting effectively dissolves the main mass of the building, apart from the projecting white fins and bays, which also act as giant shading baffles.

Opposite Vines creep up vertical pergolas, softening the face of the building and providing, as in tropical forests, the first solar filter.

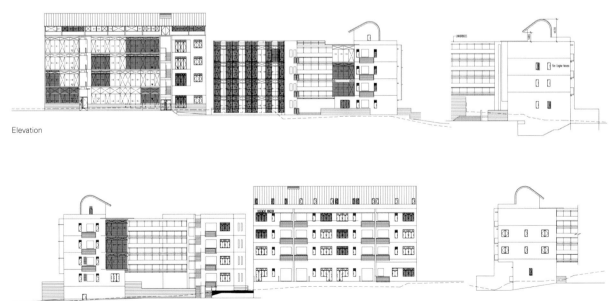

Elevation

Elevation

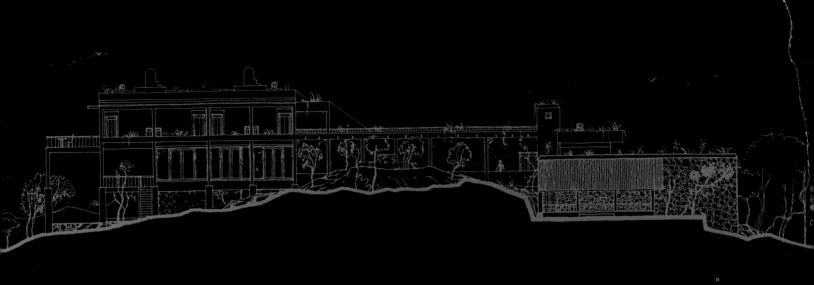

Anura Ratnavibushana

Anura Ratnavibushana (born Galle, Sri Lanka, 1940) grad-
uated from the Institute of Practical Technology, Moratuwa
(1961–63) and the Royal Danish Academy of Fine Arts,
Copenhagen (1967-69). As a student he worked at Edward
Reid & Begg (ER&B) from 1963 to 1967, under Geoffrey
Bawa, Ulrik Plesner, and ER&B partner and engineer Dr K
Poologasundaram. He travelled extensively in Scandinavia,
Europe, USSR and USA before returning to Sri Lanka in 1970
to work as Bawa's personal assistant. He also became a
partner in Design Group 5, working with them from 1970-72.
Ratnavibushana worked at ER&B with Bawa for a further
eight years. From 1980 to 1997 he worked at Mihindu
Keertiratne Associates. He established his own practice in
1997. Important completed works with ER&B include the Steel
Corporation Pavilion, Colombo (1965, designed with ANS
Kulasinghe); the Sri Lankan Pavilion, Expo 70, Osaka, Japan
(1970); the State Mortgage Bank, Colombo (1978); Library,
Chunnakkam (1972); and Library, Jaffna College, Vadukottai
(1974). Important completed works with Mihindu Keertiratne
Associates include the Mahaweli Centre, Colombo (1985);
the Law Students' Hostel, Rajagiriya (1988); interiors, Citadel
Hotel, Kandy (1987, 1992); and the Tangerine Beach Hotel
Spa, Kalutatara (2004). Important completed works as
Anura Ratnavibushana include the Museum for SWRD
Bandaranaike, Colombo (1994); Monument for Vijaya
Kumaratunga, Katunayeke (1995); Architect's House & Studio,
Battaramulle (1997); CEB Circuit Bungalow, Samanalaweva
(1999); Ranjith's House, Mt Lavinia (2001); Horagolla Library,
Horagolla (2001); Ayurveda Pavilions, Jetwing Hotel,
Negombo (2003); and interiors, Citadel Hotel, Kandy (2003).
Ratnavibushana's work has been published in *Architectural
Review, Casa Vogue* (1993), *MIMAR* (1989), *KIRA* (1994),
and *World Architecture* (1999).

Essay and project descriptions by Anoma Pieris

Anura Ratnavibushana belongs to a generation of Sri Lankan architects who grew up in the post-independence era, unburdened by the legacy of Victorian architectural norms. His education is symptomatic of this history, a first degree in Sri Lanka followed by a professional degree in Denmark. His Steel Corporation Pavilion (designed with ANS Kulasinghe) at the 1965 Industrial Exhibition in Colombo illustrates his early embrace of Modernism, with its form reminiscent of Vladimir Tatlin's Monument to the Third International. Exposure to the sculptural and figurative geometries of Scandinavian design, and its acute sensitivity to both natural and industrial materials have had a lasting effect on his work.

On returning to Sri Lanka in 1970, Ratnavibushana worked as an assistant to Geoffrey Bawa and became a flag-bearer for the vernacular revival. Confronted with the gentler tradition of the island's vernacular architecture, which had captured his mentor's imagination, his work took on a muted and fluid expression and, under the guidance of the partnership of Bawa and Danish architect Ulrik Plesner, Ratnavibushana studied the nuances of rural architectural traditions. With his increasing enchantment with the vernacular, the bold shapes and colours of his European experience were displaced into furniture design and into private fantasies explored in architecture. His own houses at Lunawa (1982) and Battaramulle, Colombo (1997), his house for his brother Ranjith (2001) and the Aryasingha House in Sri Jayawardenepura (1995) can be described as secret houses. Their flat banal façades obscure a play of rich cubist geometries within. Triangulated lampshades, a sinusoidal dining table, perspex sunshades and moulded plastic furniture are juxtaposed within skilfully interwoven spaces. In these interiors, Ratnavibushana completely abandons the compositional imperatives of the picturesque to recreate stark urban experiences. By contrast, in several office buildings designed with Bawa, Ratnavibushana's Modernist rationale makes way for the spatial contiguity of vernacular expression. His lozenge-shaped State Mortgage Bank (1976-78) is one of the finest examples of an environmentally sensitive multi-storey building taking its shape from a tight urban site.

At Mihindu Keertiratne Associates during the 1980s, Ratnavibushana adopted the regional model that by then was dominating Sri Lankan architecture. His Mahaweli Centre in Colombo (1985) adapted the traditional broad-eaved, tiled roof form to a museum building, and, in doing so, inflated the scale of the vernacular program. Colour was used decoratively on the building's façade, and the rigorous cadence of the architectural elements referred to Modernist tenets. The significant difference between this architecture and its Modernist corollary was the weighty predominance of the tiled roof, an element believed to capture the essence of Sri Lankan architectural form. In subsequent buildings for the Law Students' Hostel, Rajagiriya (1988),

Ratnavibushana continued to contain his playful geometries within this overpoweringly formal gesture.

With Ratnavibushana's translation of vernacular derivatives into a modern architectural language, he struggled with the contemporary dilemma that faced many Sri Lankan architects who sought to rationalise a romantic and additive building tradition. Whereas many architects used the new vernacular as a scenographic setting for traditional peasant objects, which they re-introduced as *objets d'art*, Ratnavibushana worked against this practice. He consistently transformed familiar shapes and forms with new materials. The tenacity of his desire to innovate absolved him of the colonial residue which had attached itself to this particular style, and it provided him with a new direction for exploration. In Ratnavibushana's most recent projects, one sees the resolution of this split subjectivity as cubist geometries re-emerge in the building form, and colour seeps into the materials and structures. The Modernism, which had been suppressed in paying homage to the vernacular, has re-surfaced in the CEB Circuit Bungalow, Samanalaweva (1999) and Horagolla Library (2001) in a moody symphony of earth-coloured geometries. From the vernacular, Ratnavibushana takes a language of repetitive frames, which draws the landscape into the building. He employs a deliberate choreography of spatial relationships, discarding sentimental ambience for a bolder architecture that is extremely personal in expression. With his design for an Ayurveda Village, at the Jetwing Hotel in Negombo (2003), in a curious inversion of his previous approach, the vernacular begins to inform a complex interior landscape of small additive forms. Throughout these transformations the principle of tectonic composition persists as a critical agenda which shapes, connects, and brings new materials into focus.

The material and tectonic inventiveness endemic to the Bauhaus tradition sets Ratnavibushana apart from many of his fellow architects. Equally it dispels the misconception that architects in South Asia are limited in their capacity to transform architectural templates, and resort to the vernacular due to a lack of resources. Small businesses, both flexible and enterprising, are replete in Asian cities and provide a healthy laboratory for custom-made architecture. Pragmatism, cheap labour and face to face contact provide a forgiving environment for inventiveness, while their success depends on a deeper cultural imprint shared by designer and producer. It is in this spirit that Ratnavibushana has produced his most exploratory work in a range of small projects, such as the Vijay Kumaranatunga memorial, Katunayeke (1995) and the Bandaranaike commemorative exhibition at the BMICH, Colombo (1996). In these architectural vignettes, the diversity of Anura Ratnavibushana's work is strikingly apparent. And more importantly, his most recent work registers Sri Lanka's tense history with a reticent and sombre aesthetic that reflects the national experience.

Ranjith's House

Year of completion 2002
Location Mt Lavinia, Sri Lanka
Architect Anura Ratnavibushana

Anura Ratnavibushana's most ingenious example of a secret house, one that has the quality of stealth, is for his brother Ranjith, wife Dayani and daughter Dayathri. It is entered through an obliquely positioned entrance in a narrow laneway off the busy Galle Road at Mt Lavinia. The entrance is dark grey and constricted through a barred gateway, heightening the surprise of the soaring interior. Flanking a triple height gallery, this three-bedroom house occupies three levels cleverly pieced together on the narrow site. The stairs rise incrementally across the various levels and ultimately open onto a roof terrace with a spectacular view of urban roofscapes and the Indian Ocean. Self-built by the client, the interior is finished with a dark grey hand-cut cement render, which plunges the spaces into a cool skylit ambience, contrasting sharply with the white light of the urban street outside.

In this house, one sees the delicate hand of an architect who has carefully articulated specific surface areas. He has integrated colour into the render of small service spaces in order to enhance their modest dimensions, and the upper walls of the gallery are clad in timber to soften their impact and to capture the dappled light from above. Pieces of furniture such as the sinusoidal dining table first designed by Anura Ratnavibushana for his Lunawa House (1982) reappear in metal and glass. Built-in furniture such as vanity tops, shelves and seats give the design a plasticity typical of cost-saving vernacular practices, while an industrial touch is added by Ratnavibushana's lamps, handrails and loose furniture.

Above and right The dark grey cement render and the glowing timber of the upper walls form a coolly austere palette within a cubic volume.

Opposite A description of complex volume, the double-height of the living room becomes a viewing room of the internal articulations of circulation through a hollowed out volume.

Horagolla Public Library

Year of completion 2001
Location Horagolla, Sri Lanka
Architect Anura Ratnavibushana

Designed for Chandrika Kumaratunga, President of Sri Lanka, as a gift to the youth and constituents of her electorate, the Horogalla Public Library is an extensive complex designed in a pragmatic Modern idiom. The structure has a reinforced concrete frame with plastered brick walls and grey machine-cut cement floors. Quite unlike the colonial institutions of the past, with their bright white exteriors and red tile roofs, Anura Ratnavibushana has used a muted vocabulary: earth-toned exterior render and unpainted interiors. The use of colour integrated cement-render at an institutional scale expands Anura Ratnavibushana's experimentation in this new medium, while reducing the maintenance costs of a rural public building. The roof of the library is broken up into areas of clay roof tiles, with exposed rafters reminiscent of vernacular roofs interspersed with flat roof terraces insulated with wild grass. The resulting forms are variegated, unlike the more homogeneous expressions of Ratnavibushana's previous regionalist-inspired institutional designs. The driving design objective is to experiment with that aspect so critical to the introspective activities of a library, the interior. Dark, dim voluminous spaces, conducive to study, are created. Indeed the complex inspires a sense of quietude, its sombre exterior blending into the rural surroundings. Carefully placed openings bring piercing shafts of light into the reading rooms. The choice of an atypical architectural expression - clothing a Modernist structure in vernacular associations – is a bold move for the architect, and is strongly reminiscent of the processes of defamiliarization through which the concept of critical regionalism was first argued. Yet the Horagolla Library has the characteristics of an experiment, both in programme and materials, which suggests a departure from regionalist roots and an embarkation on a new, exploratory path.

Opposite Contrasting with the brilliant light-filled entry, a tall volume vents the spaces below, and establishes the dark introspective atmosphere of a library.

Right The component posts of an upstairs balcony describe timeless simplicity, and provide the essential spatial requirement of the tropics: cool, dark shade.

Below At ground level, a post and beam structure and an earth-toned palette is the elemental recipe of this ordered response to the perception of a public building in a local community.

Jetwing Hotel (Ayurveda Pavilions)

Year of completion 2002
Location Negombo, Sri Lanka
Architect Anura Ratnavibushana

Whereas many of the hotels and resorts along Sri Lanka's coast recreate and project a colonial ambience for Western tourists, the Ayurveda pavilions and spas are a relatively recent introduction of a vernacular practice into the tourist industry. Ayurveda, the practice of indigenous medicine, is common to South Asia, and is widely prevalent in rural and agrarian communities. It is dependent on the knowledge and use of the medicinal properties of indigenous herbs.

Inserted into the congested and busy tourist precinct of Negombo's multi-storey hotel strip just north of Colombo, Anura Ratnavibushana's garden village design operates by providing a serene oasis in the midst of the town's hustle and bustle. The organic layout of small self-contained units clustered around courtyards is interspersed with several fountains and water features, which are innovatively integrated into the design. The project presents an austere simplicity quite unlike its luxurious resort counterparts. It offers the bare 'scaffolding' necessary for a contemplative and therapeutic form of treatment. Privacy is created through the skilful manipulation of fifteen to eighteen units designed at the scale of small rural dwellings. The entire complex uses reinforced concrete framed structures and masonry walls, with earth toned exteriors and ochre pigmented interior walls encouraging the clustered forms to merge easily into the landscape. Here, Ratnavibushana reverts to a regionalist vocabulary of pitched roofs with exposed roof timbers and clay roof tiles creating a common language for the pool, restaurant and clinic. However, Modernist rigour, evident in the visual geometry of the entire master plan and the very deliberate architectural solutions, prevents the picturesque dissolution of the project's formal intent.

The Ayurveda project highlights the possibility of developing alternative models for tourist facilities, alternatives that draw from the rural architecture of the surrounding villages, so that they do not appear inimical to their context in form and scale. The challenge taken up in Ratnavibushana's project is to achieve this without resorting to sentimental replications of an existing vernacular.

Opposite Gable roofed gateways in the high 'compound' walls of the guest pavilions have a curiously Eastern Asiatic flavour.

Above The restaurant terrace, with deep overhead beams in close succession, forms an exaggerated pergola. The western wall is punctuated by circular cut-outs: a reference to walls seen in traditional Chinese gardens walls.

CEB Circuit Bungalow

Year of completion 1999
Location Samanalaweva, Sri Lanka
Architect Anura Ratnavibushana

The Samanalaweva bungalow is one of Anura Ratnavibushana's most elegant designs, its clean lines and daring cantilevers celebrate the innovative structural approaches available to the Modernist tradition. This circuit bungalow (a colonial term for the practice of providing small private establishments for the executives of private companies) is for the engineers and officials of the Ceylon Electricity Board. Located on a remote site, steeped in folk legend, the bungalow overlooks one of Sri Lanka's symbols of modern engineering, the Samanalaweva Reservoir. It is designed in the tradition of the 'stealth container', concealing riches within. This has become a signature approach in Ratnavibushana's recent projects.

A low verandah-like entrance belies the length and scale of the three-storey bungalow. Approached along winding rural roads, the bungalow is discreetly positioned as one of the many 'houses by the road': quite unlike its colonial precedent. One enters the bungalow through an enclosed skylit stairway tunnel painted in a golden yellow ochre. This space acts as the entrance hall leading to the living and bedroom levels behind. The movement inside and upward opens up the visual circumference of the site, giving spectacular views of the reservoir. The cantilevered slabs, supported by a reinforced concrete frame, are the strongest structural elements, creating a feeling of suspension in the forest canopy. The concrete roof slabs are engineered to withstand the extreme windy conditions, and these surface areas have been planted with wild grass and foliage so that they blend naturally into the surrounding terrain. The grey painted walls and machine-cut grey cement floors recede into the hillside and, with the large picture windows, they allow the site to enter the space within. The forest setting and the bungalow's dark tones create an unusual ambience of being nestled in the hillside, and the warm timber surfaces and mahogany furniture, designed in a minimalist style, enhance this sense of containment. Out on the terraces the experience is quite the opposite. Unprotected, one has the sense of being perched precariously on the edge of the world.

Anura Ratnavibushana demonstrates remarkable talent and versatility with this unique project. The CEB Bungalow realises a clever orchestration of varied experiences across a provocative site.

Left A terraced landscape in a wild terrain – the slabs of the rooftop form a cultivated mosaic hovering above the mountainside.

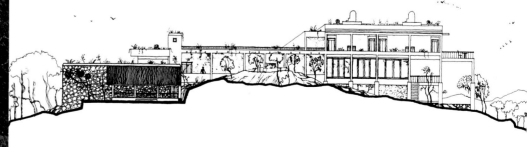

North elevation

South elevation

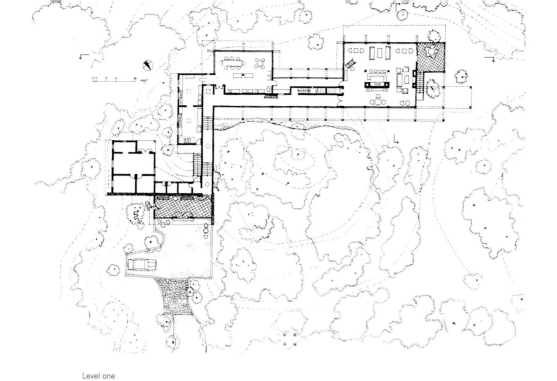

Level one

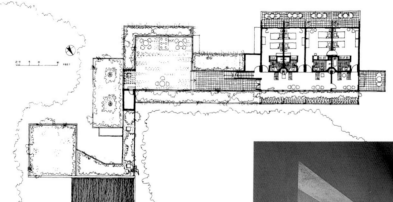

Level two

Opposite The roof terrace offers spectacular views of the distant landscape, in the manner of a ceremonial plateau or rooftop temple. The eccentric sculptured forms have a practical purpose, concealing service vents, flues and skylights.

Below The architectural vocabulary is restrained and archetypal: the rhythms of post and beam, the rendered plain walls and the polished concrete floor are the language of Modernism; now fundamental to the material practices of the region.

Kevin Low

Kevin Mark Low (born Johore, Malaysia, 1964) graduated
from the University of Oregon (USA) in 1988 and the
Massachusetts Institute of Technology in 1991. He worked
at SRG Partnership (1988) and GBD Architects (1989) in
Oregon, and lectured at MIT's School of Architecture and
Planning in 1990. Returning to Malaysia in 1992, Low joined
GDP Architects in Kuala Lumpur, where he worked as a
design architect (1992-94), design associate (1995 –2000)
and design director (2001-02). He left GDP to establish
his own firm, 'small projects' in 2002. Low teaches at the
University of Malaya. Important completed projects in
Malaysia with GDP include the Yong House, Taman Duta
(1993); Garden Memorial, Ipoh, Perak (1998); Minco
corporate offices, Petaling Jaya (1999); Lone Pine Hotel,
Penang (2000); Nada's House, Sierramas (2000); Master Plan,
Kampung Cina, Terengganu (2000); and Master Plan, Sentul,
Malaysia (2002). Important works as 'small projects' include
the Lightwell House, Kuala Lumpur (2000-); Safari Roof House,
Kuala Lumpur (2002-); Louvrebox House, Gita Bayu (2004);
Ventblock House (2002-); Brickwall House, Kuala Lumpur
(2003); Lightbox House, Petaling Jaya (2004-); and Brickyard
House, Petaling Jaya (2004-).

Essay and project descriptions by Anoma Pieris

Kevin Low's inner-city projects in Kuala Lumpur have a phenomenological agenda of reclaiming the direct effects of textures often lost in modern urbanism.

In the period after the 1997 recession, when many small design firms in Malaysia found themselves in dire financial straits, Kevin Low's tenacious aesthetic and selective approach to projects has earned him opportunities to experiment and innovate, despite very limited budgets. Low's work raises important questions about definitions of regionalism, currently polarized between traditional forms and climatic responses. He produces a gritty, yet sensitive, vocabulary for a Modernist vernacular. Low's approach to design is strongly influenced by his education at Massachusetts Institute of Technology and its Aga Khan Program, which, during the 1990s, developed a strong non-Western agenda in design teaching. Combined with his work-experience in the USA, this education has given his architecture a tectonic focus. The clarity of his structural expression, honesty to materials and keen attention to detail demonstrates the rigour of this early 1990s approach, which reduced formal agendas to their kit of parts, and explored collage, systemic structure and regional construction methods.

In Low's work one can read two interpretations of the tectonic: sensitive interventions into the urban fabric, borrowing materials and textures from surrounding architecture; and strong formal gestures made on sites where space and terrain provide opportunities for object-making. His architecture is not derived from traditional forms or cultural icons, but from his sensitivity to the material at hand in the Malaysian building industry and a sympathetic appreciation of the local climate. In doing so, Low's designs draw on Modernist and Postmodern vocabularies: of the engineer and the bricoleur. And the naming of his projects expresses the deliberate instrumentality governing their design.

The Lightwell House (2000-), the Brickwall House (2003) and the Brickyard House (2004-) are designed as a series of urban rooms that capture the shifting of light over the day. There is an evanescent quality to these spaces, created by the passing shadows of soft foliage and slender saplings against their textured walls. Fair-faced bricks, fired but not wire-cut, give these projects a softness absent from the pristine spaces of familiar Modernisms. Low's inner-city projects have a phenomenological agenda of reclaiming the direct effects of textures often lost in modern urbanism. The restrained lightness of his touch is evident in many small interventions, such as the forms of a perforated stair, a terrace awning stretcher, shelving, and other fixed furniture which has been introduced into his projects. The unfinished quality of the architecture compensates for the varying degree of skill of Malaysian workmen, the haphazard process of construction (where a project must be divided between multiple sub-contractors) and the processes of weathering that inevitably mark buildings in the tropics. Low's objective is to capture the passage of time as a part of the tectonic memory of a project, so that its marks can be read

in the way that one might follow the temporal transformations of the natural landscape.

Low's more formal explorations of residential design are located outside Kuala Lumpur, within the boundaries of former palm-oil plantations. The undulating hills of these agricultural sites have been claimed for high-income housing and have provided Malaysian architects with an experimental ground for Modernism. Low's design for a house on the Sierramas estate (2000, for GDP Architects) clearly demonstrates the kit of parts approach with its light repetitive structures and a playful use of sections. In his latest projects, the use of pre-cast cement vent blocks gives the projects an almost ruthless spareness, although the slender lines of the structure belie any comparison with Brutalism. With the floating roof used in the Safari Roof House, Kuala Lumpur (currently under construction), the cross ventilation, enabled by the separation of the roof from the walls, is a strong gesture towards developing an environmentally sensitive response.

Whereas interventions in the hard urban landscape have been soft and diffused in their expression, Low intervenes in the gentle scape of natural hillsides with bold lines and strong contrasts, which mould geometric spaces against the undulations of the surroundings. The austere quality of the interior spaces, the inventive use of simple and inexpensive materials, and the clarity of structural lines create a habitable and appropriate architecture. Whereas his urban architecture conceives of the house as a series of garden rooms which blur the distinctions between inside and outside, his architecture outside Kuala Lumpur achieves this porosity by welcoming the natural elements. In gated communities such as Sierramas, where a more ostentatious architecture is common, Low's projects exist in stark contrast to their neighbours. What we can see in Kevin Low's architecture is the emergence of a vernacular in the making: a *lingua franca* derived from contemporary conditions, which diffuses more formal Modernist approaches to architecture.

Brickwall House

Year of completion 2003
Location Kuala Lumpur, Malaysia
Architect Kevin Low

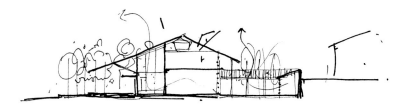

With this project, Kevin Low continues his strategy of softening the urban compaction of constricted sites by introducing the soft and warm tones of brickwork. The project builds on the vocabulary of brick walls and courtyards which had been introduced in the Lightwell House (2000-). It reconfigures the street boundaries and occupies the entire site by wrapping the spaces in a red brick envelope. The bricks used in this project are fired, but not wire-cut, giving them a weathered appearance, blunting the geometric edges of the urban frame.

The project is a renovation of a double storey, post-war semi-detached house, giving Low an opportunity to explore his predilection for an incremental geometry sensitively inserted into an existing structure. The design builds a contiguity of spaces and materials by extending the tile roof over the front entry wall to resemble the blade thin porches of Malaysian workshops. The roof is extended once again at the centre of the house. It shelters a wet kitchen, which occupies a central courtyard garden, a celebration of the Malaysian typology and the way of life it embodies. The Brickwall House has the experimental quality evident in Low's own house. It suggests the system of bricolage, by which the architect brings together the old and the new, responding to fresh possibilities and associations as they make their appearance. In an enclosed urban site the desire to enhance the quality of direct light on material surfaces predominates, and the rough surfaces of the red brick emanate a warm glow. Low's willingness to abandon the Modernist imperative of the *tabula rasa* when the project calls for a more intuitive and integrated architecture, demonstrates his confidence in responding to specific sites and to construct through phenomenological experience.

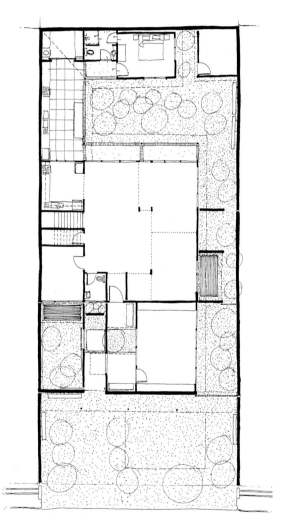

Opposite The deft insertion of new brick walls and concrete-block screens; a new ground landscape of random paving, pebbles and stepping stones; and the inclusion of specimen trees, creates an exterior environment of rich tactility, warmth and visual variety.

Level one

Lightwell House

Year of commencement 2000 (ongoing construction)
Location Kuala Lumpur, Malaysia
Architect Kevin Low

Kevin Low's house and office in Jalan Tenggiri encapsulates his personal interpretation of architecture as a process which unravels gradually around a specific site, giving it material form. The house, originally an urban terrace house at the end of a cul-de-sac, has been transformed completely. Low removed the internal walls and designed the whole site as a series of garden rooms. The house walls extend to the boundary and reference the red brick of the nearby storage yards, anchoring the project in its urban context. On entering through the boundary wall, one moves through a series of spaces – some completely open to the sky and others act as courtyards – to spaces deep within the structure. Trees, chosen carefully and planted in specific outdoor spaces, tie the project together: the cherry tree outside, the frangipani marking the far corner and the *ficus triangularis* next to the dining terrace. The white epoxy floor inside the house presents a bright contrast to the red brick of the pathways and terraces, defining potential geometries and giving the interior a light floating quality.

Low is content in knowing that his house is unfinished. His method of building (co-ordinating several sub-contractors) calls for an incremental approach that he feels is suited to the low-tech low-budget industry with which he is dealing. He works intuitively with the material, respecting its temporal nature and anticipating the changes that may take place with time. In fact, he delights in the transformations of the various rooms at different times of day – in the white heat of the afternoon or the darkness of a sudden monsoon shower – enjoying it all the more, as he works in one or the other of the spaces.

Above A corner of the oddly shaped site at the end of a cul-de-sac, becomes a location of formal and material intersection: a collection of pots, an 'as-found' art piece.

Right Weathering in the tropics is an organic process. Materials age quickly, and the rapid growth of trees, vines and shrubs adds to this rapid gaining of character. In the garden rooms of the Lightwell House, such 'weathering' becomes the sign of the architectural forms softening, to appear artlessly natural.

Level two

Level one

Above The dining room's aspect extends beyond the eaves: its space expands into each garden room beyond.

Opposite The terracotta tiled floor passes from inside to out, as does the plane of the ceiling above. The courtyard beyond appears as a skylight rather than an outdoor space.

Louvrebox House

Year of completion 2004
Location Gita Bayu, Malaysia
Architect Kevin Low

Opposite The front door and entry sequence of the Louvrebox House is a reverie in materiality, and in point, line and plane.

The Louvrebox House sits in the undulating landscape of Gita Bayu, south of Kuala Lumpur, a former plantation converted into a gated community. The house, occupying the smallest and narrowest lot in the estate, is a three storey rectangular box, twenty-six metres in length and five metres wide. A 2.2 metre wide lap pool flanks the house along a side garden. The strong geometry of the house contrasts sharply with the softness of the surrounding context, but first appearances are deceptive. On entering the long rectangular spaces, the porosity of the envelope diffuses the architectural boundaries, allowing the house to become subsumed by nature. A glass box, acting as a lobby, leads to a concrete plinth area reserved for entertainment. As the site slips sharply away, the ground plane appears to cantilever. The remaining spaces, wrapped in panels of aluminium louvres, are suspended above the entertainment plinth giving the house its predominant expression of a louvred box. Calculated to optimize the balance between views to the landscape and desired levels of privacy, the louvres act as a living skin which modulates heat gain and humidity. Characteristically, Kevin Low introduces a precise industrial aesthetic into a picturesque setting and, ignoring the 'tropical vernacular' idiom, heightens our sensitivity to his choice of materials by the technique of contrast.

Opposite The Louvrebox
House has a linear 'thinness'
and a pared-back structural
minimalism, with elegantly
simple glazing and a
rigorously austere palette
of materials.

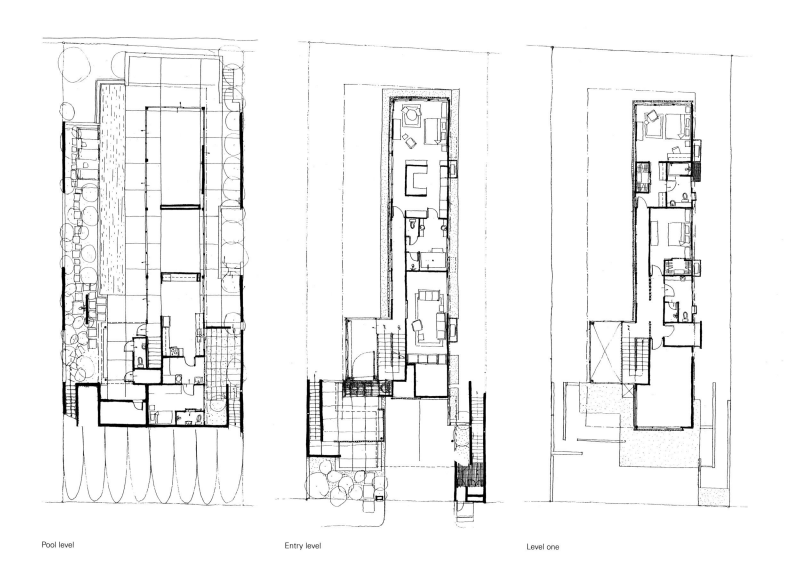

Pool level

Entry level

Level one

Left The glazed stair-bay sits behind a floating steel canopy and breeze-block screen. The house has the quality of a Miesian pavilion, adapted to respond to tropical heat, humidity and rain.

Right Viewed from the south east in the early evening, the Louvrebox House appears as a glowing set of boxes beneath the dark protecting shadow of its floating roof.

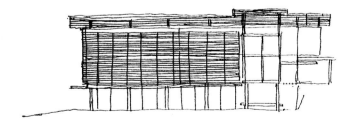

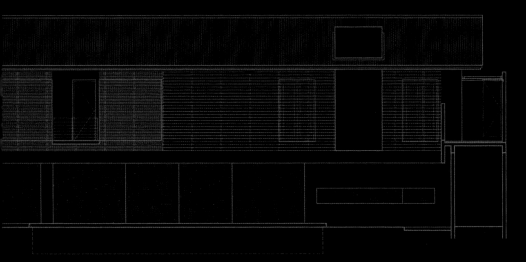

Andra Matin Architect

Isandra Matin (born Bandung, Indonesia, 1962) graduated from Parahyangan University, Bandung, in 1988. After working in Jakarta for Pt. Grahacipta Hadiprana-Architect from 1990 to 1998, he established Andra Matin Architect (AMA) in Jakarta in 1998. Avianti Armand (born Jakarta, Indonesia, 1969) graduated from University of Indonesia, Jakarta, in 1992. She worked for Pt. Grahacipta Hadiprana-Architect from 1994 to 1998 before joining AMA. Matin and Armand have taught at the University of Indonesia (Jakarta), Parahyangan University (Bandung), the Technological Institute of Bandung (ITB) and Tarumanegara University (Jakarta). Both have been active participants in Jakarta's Arsitek Muda Indonesia (Young Indonesian Architect), a forum comprised of practicing architects, students and academics, established in 1989. AMA's work has been exhibited in Den Haag and Jakarta. Important completed projects include Le Bo Ye Graphic Design Office, South Jakarta (1998); Paper Gallery, Bandung, West Java (1999); Gedung Dua8 Ethnology Museum, Kemang, Jakarta (1999); Ak'sara Book Store and Prodåk Homeware, Kemang, Jakarta (2001); Ramzy Gallery and Fiori Beauty Salon, Bangka, Jakarta (2002); and House in Cipete, Jakarta (2002). The firm's work has been published in *Architecture Asia, ASRI, d+a* (Singapore), *ID* (Singapore), *Kompas, LARAS* and *Space* (Singapore).

Essay and project descriptions by Amanda Achmadi

Working mostly in Jakarta, Andra Matin Architect (AMA) perceives the city's chaotic urban context and current architecture as something to resist and deconstruct, rather than to deny or take for granted. AMA's elegant compositions and clear tectonics are comforting when viewed against Jakarta's recent monstrous typologies of towering neo-Classical and Mediterranean styled housing estates and commercial buildings, or when compared with the predictable symbolic repro-duction of Indonesian vernacular architecture seen in governmental buildings and public institutions. AMA's design approach is informed strongly by the subtle compositions and restrained modernity of works by such Japanese architects as Fumihiko Maki and Kengo Kuma. Beneath this visual language, however, lies a deliberate attempt to re-inscribe the possibility of and the potential for contem-porary architecture within Jakarta's tropical climate and complex urban society. AMA sees its role as showing the urban middle class other ways of living in the city.

Andra Matin and Avianti Armand spent the early part of their careers working for one of Indonesia's most established architectural firms, Pt. Grahacipta Hadiprana, a practice with a strong reputation for its concern with 'Indonesian accent' – the aesthetics of the country's ubiquitous indigenous idioms in arts, handicrafts and architecture. For many practising architects, the picturesque strength of this 'Indonesian accent' diverts engagement from more daring, conceptually-driven spatial experiments. They believe that architectural design has become a form of mediocre building production, confined by the glib staging and stylization of these perceived Indonesian arts. When Matin and Armand began their own practice, they engaged with the indigenous traditions, but through an interpretation of those tradition's spatial qualities. They combined this engagement with ongoing questions about space and urbanity in contemporary Jakarta: a diverse society immersed by rapid flows of information, characterized by the placelessness of the urban middle class, and a struggle to define an identity between bourgeois lifestyle and the desperate living conditions of the marginalized urban poor.

AMA's mission is to position architecture as an active cell of the city, considering the impact of building scale, language and activity within its context. AMA experiments with combined zones of activity which can enable interactions between different backgrounds of users, and which can spatially articulate notions of a city's civic society. The Le Bo Ye Graphic Design project (1999) introduced AMA to a specific segment of middle and upper class Jakarta: the arts and humanities professionals, who were eager to re-imagine a new architectural experience and still live in the city. Among them was ethnologist and documentary filmmaker Dea Sudarman, who was to commission AMA to design a museum and library for East Indonesian artefacts and culture. This project, Gedung Dua8 (1999),

was realized as a laboratory for art observers, artists and other related professionals: an inspiring space previously absent from Jakarta's shopping mall and traffic jam lifestyle.

AMA is especially concerned with the lack of accessibility of most of Jakarta's urban spaces, a condition exacerbated by the lack of dialogue between architecture and urban context; a phenomenon that increasingly is turning Jakarta's urban spaces into residual spaces, and from which each building seeks to protect itself. To counter this, AMA has closely explored the design of the site boundary, public access and pedestrian movement in Gedung Dua8, combining modern geometric volumes with the kampung characteristics of permeable and accessible space.

AMA considers tropical design as a field of experiment, rather than as a predicted and finished style, commonly identified by the reproduction of perceived vernacular architectural forms (regardless of their origin, socio-economic roles and significance), such as exposed wood construction, complex pitched roof formations, and ironically, by a profusion of air conditioning outlets. AMA prefers to adapt their geometric compositions to the tropical climate –manipulating the building envelope to enable internal air move-ment, to establish the correct solar orientation, to alleviate the high humidity and to protect from the tropical rainfall.

With their attempts to reinterpret the 'local', AMA continually questions its own methods. Should AMA, for example, only reinterpret and contest the 'local', while the 'modern' style, and indeed modernity itself, is perceived as complete and 'immortal'? Their most recent Jakarta projects, the Ramzy Gallery and Fiori Beauty Lounge, Bangka (2002) and the House in Cipete (2002), reflect this ongoing struggle, where more daring compositions of texture and volumetric quality have been produced. The House in Cipete offers an ingenious proposition for a typically dense housing precinct, and the Ramzy Gallery and Fiori Beauty Lounge offers an alternative to the unmitigated ugliness and visual pollution of the busy commercial strips throughout Jakarta.

Andra Matin Architect conceives contemporary design as a spatial formulation. At a social level it resists the polarizing legacy of Jakarta's modern urban and architectural history, while at the aesthetic level it pursues inventive climatic responses through space and composition, through plays of texture and light, and through the permeability of building enclosure. In a city where most contemporary architectural projects turn away from their urban contexts with bourgeois image-making, massive walls and towering gates, and where urban realms are increasingly being transformed into negative spaces, AMA refuses to be compliant, and insists on imagining and constructing dynamic engagements between archi-tecture, a multi-cultural urban society, and the 'becoming' of Jakarta.

Le Bo Ye Graphic Design

Year of completion 1999
Location South Jakarta, Indonesia
Architect Andra Matin Architect

Le Bo Ye Graphic Design, AMA's first work, was a low budget project that boldly delivered the firm's formal language. While a renovation and extension of an existing structure, the project inserted new elements – light, distance and wall permeability – as key space-making tools. From the street, the project maintains the building scale and roof typology of the existing structure and the neighbourhood. Horizontally-laid timber battens cover a row of windows on the building's upper floor: this creates adequate privacy for the office and acoustic separation from the busy traffic of the neighbourhood below, without blocking light or the view. A planar wall directs visitors to the main entrance, which is located at the building's rear in a cubic two-level volume, serving as a lobby and multi-functional room. Two thirds of the upper part of the volume, including its glass ceiling, is completely enclosed by horizontally-laid timber battens, and this striated surface filters sunlight while casting a changing pattern of shadow lines and rays of light across the floor and walls. A setback timber-framed glass window, which can be fully opened, encloses the lower third of the mass, and the overall treatment of the building boundary enables airflow into the space inside. The lobby design enables office workers and visitors to view and engage with the site and its landscape, an experience ignored in Jakarta's conventional office buildings. This breathing volume shows that Jakarta's climate can be liveable, once building enclosures and landscape elements are judiciously arranged to facilitate air-flow, thus moderating the harsh temperatures and humidity.

Right The timber-battened glass box can be seen as a lantern, or indeed as a symphony of sticks. The timber cladding of the gallery is used, instead of eaves, to provide permanent shade.

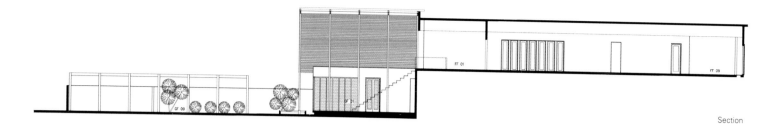

Section

Left and right The wonderful volume of the gallery can be seen as a 'shade house', demonstrating tectonic clarity and externalizing the 'great hall' or grand space. Significantly, this gallery is not a 'verandah' but a 'room'.

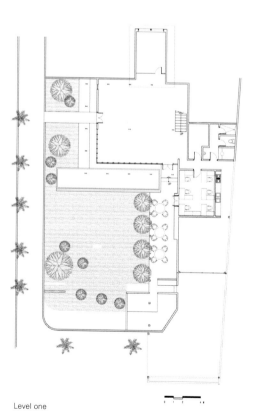

Level one

Gedung Dua8 Ethnology Museum

Year of completion 1999
Location Jakarta, Indonesia
Architect Andra Matin Architect

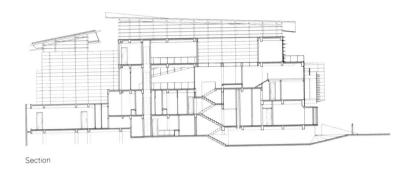

Section

For most contemporary Indonesians, knowledge of indigenous cultures has long been delivered as a set of standardized interpretations of ancient heritages; just as it has been reproduced, in authorised form, by the 'Indonesia in Miniature Park' in East Jakarta. For the Gedung Dua8 project, AMA resisted such a disciplined cultural formulation when they worked with a research team that continues to study the ethnology of the eastern Indonesia, oblivious to the official version of what is meant by 'ancient'. AMA and the client transformed an unremarkable building site into an architectural field where ideas of culture and possibilities of cultural interpretation could be re-inscribed. Their task was to provide spaces for ongoing learning (a library), exhibition and observation (museum), discussion (amphitheatre and multi-function room) and development (research office). The completed complex consists of three buildings: two existing buildings whose structures were maintained, and a new central connecting building. Internally, a contemplative and less formal learning space is in contrast to the common utilitarian expression of education facilities in Jakarta. The complex's boundary, in the form of a sloping landscaped platform, was designed to minimize the separation between the neighbourhood and the building complex. Unlike a boundary wall, this piece of landscape creates a soft transition rather than massive barrier, and a pedestrian lane cuts across the site allowing the public to access and experience the museum, whether they intend to visit or are simply passing by. The pedestrian route passes an open amphitheatre located in the middle of the site, where a ramp leads visitors to the museum entrance on the first floor. The use of ramps as the main circulation system provides disabled access – long ignored in Indonesia's public buildings. The entrance space, enclosed by amphitheatre steps, a pedestrian ramp, and cut across by an enclosed ramp connecting the second and third floors, reproduces the permeability of kampung space. The interior is never thoroughly detached from the outside.

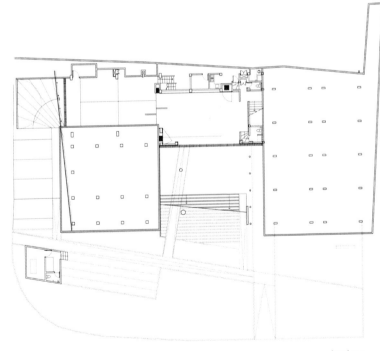

Level one

Left An open-air volume within the prismatic form of the museum is the stage for an informal auditorium space, viewed from 'primitive' seating of stones and planks.

Opposite The building's exterior is dominated by horizontal lines and planes, a reflection of the scale and location of the immediate neighbourhood and fluidity of traffic movement.

Below The concrete frame of the original building and the new link building is celebrated as an internal 3D landscape of volume.

House in Cipete

Year of completion 2002
Location Jakarta, Indonesia
Architect Andra Matin Architect

On a busy street in a dense housing area in South Jakarta, this house has a modest façade; a privacy and sound barrier which contributes positively to the streetscape. As with Gedung Dua8, AMA used a sloping landscape platform to connect the street with the first floor levels of the house. Belonging to a young couple, the house is designed to be a dynamic space providing flexibility of activity and privacy. The house comprises two aligned zones: the front contains the foyer, a guest room and a games/study room; while the rear contains a long studio space that opens onto the back garden, with a pantry at one end and a living room at the other. Bedrooms and bathrooms are located on the upper floor, while a service area is pooled at one side of the house. Dividing and connecting the two zones is a staircase and a 'light' (glass-roofed) corridor, and a permeable panel made of aligned timber slats is positioned at both ends of the corridor. This space is thus the breathing volume of the house.

The towering presence of a wall divider between house lots, a common phenomenon of Jakarta's housing districts, dominates the pool and garden landscape. AMA has converted this intimidating circumstance into a poetic context, exposing the red bricks of the neighbourhood 'relief' wall. This move creates a coarse yet pleasant texture, a humble enclosure of the site and a subtle celebration of Jakarta's urban density.

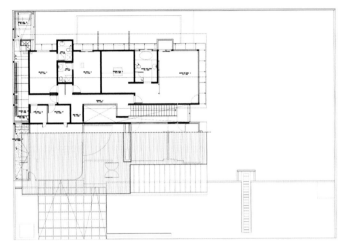

Level two

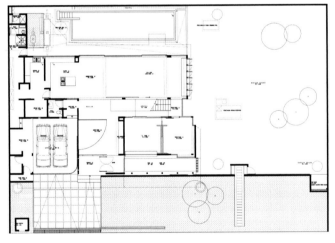

Level one

Opposite The planar proportions of the living area and studio, combined with the use of sliding frameless glass windows, provide an elegant panorama. The interior space blends spatially and visually with the pool area and the back garden.

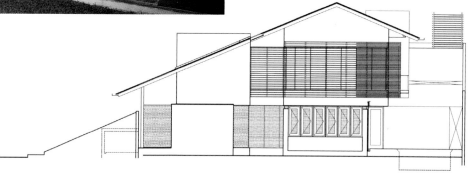

West elevation

Above The pragmatic gable roof and projecting window screens protect the exposed western façade of the house from the afternoon sun.

Right A sheer wall of glass is the only boundary between the polished floor and the swimming pool. At the western end of this light-filled living space, a dark band of deliberately delineated windows is in complete contrast to the invisible wall to the south.

Ramzy Gallery and
Fiori Beauty Salon

Year of completion 2002
Location Bangka, Jakarta, Indonesia
Architect Andra Matin Architect

Below The ramp, seen here on the southern edge of the gallery, is the archetypal vehicle for the Modernist spatial experience. The movement up or down through a space transgresses age-old notions of axiality.

Opposite The sculpted bay window is a composition of angled and vertical glass panels arranged in a random, almost Cubist pattern. The result is a piece of 'architectural art'.

On a busy commercial strip in South Jakarta, AMA was asked to convert half of an existing house into a ground floor art gallery and first floor beauty salon. With a lack of regulation, most commercial strips in Jakarta witness chaotic profusions of signage, producing characterless and, in some cases, unidentifiable streetscapes. In response, AMA explored the idea of creating architecture as signage, designing a randomly fragmented steel-framed glass window which covers the front of the building. Consisting of different sizes, angles and opacities of glass, this façade possesses an intense texture of light reflection and sunlight during day, and its interior lighting gives the building a memorable night-time presence. On this façade can be read AMA's ongoing experiments in texture and craftsmanship. Entering the gallery on the ground floor, visitors are enclosed by a combination of a glass platform and a bent surface of vertically lined timber slats, which cover the wall and the ceiling of the foyer. Here AMA restates its ongoing exploration of dynamic spatiality, through plays of building textures and ever-changing shafts of sunlight. In contrast to this intense light-modelled foyer, a calm white wall encloses the exhibition space, and a more subdued staging of space is created through the positioning of a skylight in the centre of a black painted ceiling.

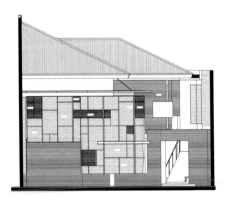

West elevation

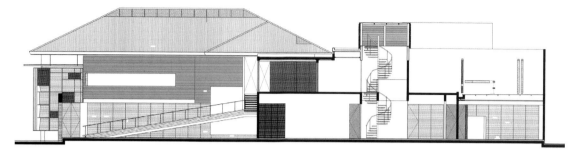

South elevation

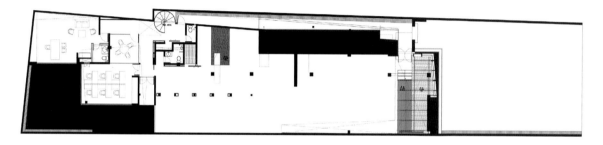

Level one

Opposite The composition of the corner window bay recalls the intricate detail and artifice of Carlo Scarpa's jewel-like shops and galleries of the late 1950's in Italy.

Right From the gallery one can view the movement of passers-by on the external ramp: a show in parallel to the works within.

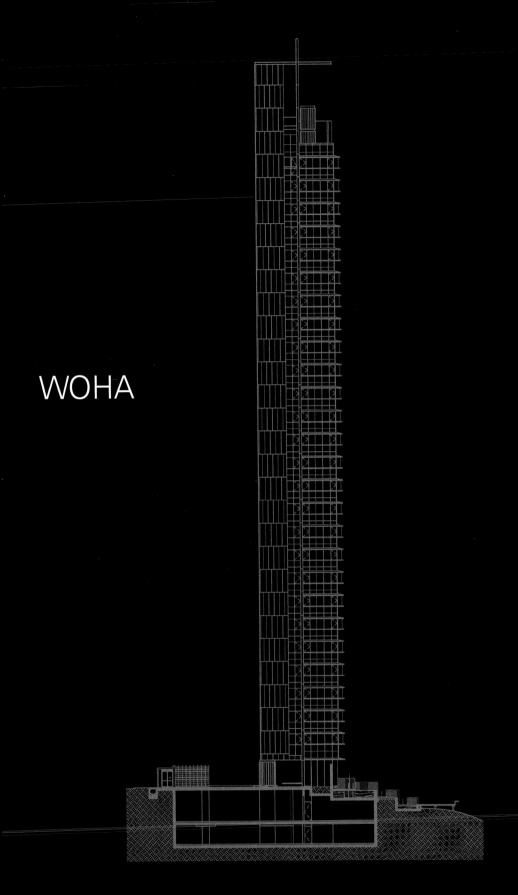

WOHA

Essay and project descriptions
by Anoma Pieris

Wong Mun Summ (born Singapore, 1962) graduated from
the National University of Singapore in 1989. As a student
he worked for William Lim Associates, and joined Kerry
Hill Architects after graduation. Richard Hassell (born Perth,
Australia, 1966) graduated from the University of Western
Australia in 1989 and immediately joined Kerry Hill Architects
in Singapore. Both Wong and Hassell had their initial training
working on resort hotels in Southeast Asia, and were made
associates at Kerry Hill Architects. Over the next five years
they worked on projects such as the Datai, Langkawi,
Malaysia and The Serai, Bali, Indonesia. In 1994 they formed
their own practice, WOHA, in Singapore. Important projects
include 12 Houses at Watten Estate Road, Singapore (1995-
1998); Conserved Shophouse at Emerald Hill Road, Singapore
(1995-1998); 3 Houses at Victoria Park Road, Singapore (1998-
2000); Church of St Mary of the Angels, Singapore (1999-2003);
House at Maple Avenue, Singapore (1999-2002); House
at Hua Guan Avenue, Singapore (1999-2002); 3 Houses at
Berrima Road, Singapore (1999-2002); No 1 Moulmein Rise,
Singapore (2000-2003); Boulevard MRT Station, Singapore
(2000-); Museum MRT Station, Singapore (2000-); Conserved
Shophouse at 175 Telok Ayer Street, Singapore (2001-2002);
House at Rochalie Drive, Singapore (2001-2003); Odeon
Towers Extension, Singapore (2001-2003); Cluster Housing
at Gilstead Road, Singapore (2002-2004); and Mixed Use
Development, Bangkok (2003-). WOHA's work has been
published in *A + U* (Japan), *Architectural Review* (UK),
Architectural Review Australia (Australia), *Singapore
Architect* (Singapore), *Architectural Record* (USA), *Phaidon
Atlas of Contemporary World Architecture* and *10x10* (vol 2).

Singapore based WOHA Architects, Australian-born Richard Hassell and Singapore-born Wong Mun Summ, demonstrate a Modernist approach to materials and technologies, adapted to a humid tropical climate. Both architects cite influences from their student years: the great Modernist architects such as Le Corbusier and Frank Lloyd Wright; then Louis Kahn, the New York Five, and Mario Botta. But this is the limit of their Modernism. WOHA's approach ultimately interrogates its own intellectual context – the regionalist discourse of the 1990s – which is framed as contextual Modernism.

Both WOHA principals attribute their elegant detailing and highly resolved planning to their training with Kerry Hill Architects, where they worked on designs for exclusive resorts, deriving a picturesque and sensual architecture from local vernacular. Critical to such work were the designs of entire contexts for specific programs, and the choreographing of movement along the visual axes which frame a site's tropical geography. Such practices generated a thorough knowledge of vernacular typologies, climatic responses, and a revival of construction methods and technologies of specific cultures. A design method evolved that required, for each project, the development of an appropriate kit of parts. In WOHA's architecture, one can now see this as an unravelling of orthodox regionalist strategies.

WOHA emerged as a practice in the final years of the Asian economic boom, just when the region was sliding into recession. It was a period when government policies and industry monopolies directed the speed and scale of architectural production, focusing on economics and pragmatics over aesthetic considerations. By the late 1990s, shrinking budgets transformed this economy, bringing the work of design architects like WOHA into focus. Unlike the formulaic apartment types and corporate models which have colonized Singapore's urban fabric, WOHA's architecture has developed a wide range of forms and abstract language, through a design process adapted to the range and scale of each project. In the post-recession climate, the inherent flexibility of their method has attracted both public and private clients, giving WOHA a reputation for sensitivity and versatility. This fresh approach has brought diverse commissions, including a religious complex, a multi-storey apartment building, and through international competition, the designs for the Boulevard and Museum MRT (Mass Rail Transit) stations (now under construction and due for completion in 2006). At the Museum Station, minimal interventions at ground level contrast with a dramatic canyon-like entry to the underground station. Reflecting pools and a courtyard create a new datum for light as well as people. By contrast, at the Boulevard Station, the intervention is above ground, with a vehicular bridge over the pedestrian access route. In each project the entire site is developed as the context for an urban architecture particularly suited to Singapore.

In WOHA's housing projects, the richness of textures and materials are organized not through the familiar picturesque approach, but by an underlying industrial sensibility. Their designs express a lightness, which contrasts markedly with the heavy colonial bungalow tradition. While their houses capture the environmental sensibilities of colonial models, their spatial qualities are transformed when translated into a contemporary aesthetic. In each house, there is a programmatic template: a self-contained circulation axis which separates public and private space. These public domestic spaces are graduated by layers which forestall the moment of discovery, preparing the observer for direct engagement with the urban context. The porosity of their building envelopes emphasizes this objective.

In an early exploration of the shophouse typology at Emerald Hill (1995-1998), WOHA refused to replicate the divisions of the familiar tube-like plan. Rather, they chose to strip it bare, exposing the interior shell and redesigning it to capture the formal relationships of an urban street. In tackling high-density housing, the most relevant dwelling type for land-scarce Singapore, WOHA reiterate this urban logic. The plans for the No 1 Moulmein Rise Apartments (2001-2003) display the same division of public and private zones that defines their one-off residential projects. Plans turn outward to establish visual connections to the city. This tactic deliberately challenges the tendency to incarcerate high-rise dwellers in hermetically sealed environments. With their award-winning entry for the Duxton Plains Public Housing competition (2002), WOHA adapted this brief to a fifty-storey apartment model, designed as nine tower blocks. Their scheme proposed new datum levels at every fifth storey from the tenth floor upwards, introducing skyparks and skystreets which combine to form sky villages for 360 families.

WOHA's vocabulary is inherently playful, but this 'easy going' approach belies a serious design agenda. While identifying a familiar typology as a point of departure, their objective is to take it apart as the form evolves. Unlike the monolithic forms and labour-intensive methods of many regionalist examples, their architecture draws on an industrial legacy, producing a lighter, more pragmatic, aesthetic designed in modular repetitive components. Once modules have been established, they are organized randomly, adapted to the specifics of context, or interrupted to accommodate the brief with a freedom that defies the Modernist desire for composition.

WOHA's strength is in their reflective conceptual approach and their fine-grained detailing, through which each project is refined into an elegant architectural expression. In a design culture where architects use a narrow repertoire of forms and materials and depend on established methods, WOHA's open-ended approach demonstrates an adventurous temperament and technological dexterity, thus allowing the firm to venture beyond regionalist imperatives.

3 Houses at Victoria Park Road

Year of completion 2000
Location Singapore
Architect WOHA

Designed as three separate units on a tight urban site, these houses provide a template for WOHA's modular matrix. The concept of the matrix, which refers to the rhythmic geometries of Paul Klee's landscapes, is manipulated in plan, in section and in the choice of building elements. Each house takes up the narrow linear form of the urban shophouse, but is set two metres apart from its neighbour. The detaching of tubular forms creates a bank of landscaping, which acts as a buffer between each unit and creates opportunities for a more permeable envelope. Seen in plan the modules are clearly marked: the same list of spaces (living, dining, entry, and pool) is reconfigured within the intricate geometry of the system and adjusted to fit into the site. The aesthetic employed borrows from the tropical regional vocabulary to develop its details, but omits the heavy base and nostalgic imagery that typically accompany its expression. By contrast, the pavilion forms are top heavy with the mass of the second storey hovering over the glazed lower level. The entire design is composed of a series of sliding screens, glazed or louvred, that present no barrier to the visual connections through the building, allowing air currents to flow easily through and up the stairwell. This project recalls the planar geometry and flexible screens of Gerrit Rietveld's Schroeder house. Screens, carefully manipulated and designed for varying degrees of opacity, determine the levels of privacy needed between the closely spaced houses. Unlike the tropical regionalist model, these townhouses have flat roofs with deep cantilevering eaves to give sun and rain protection. The proprietary louvre system imparts an industrial aesthetic, in keeping with the discipline of the tectonic system. With a rigorous exploration of environmental responses at several levels of the building envelope and the clever manipulation of space and typology, these three houses at Victoria Park Road are exemplars of WOHA's refined design rationale.

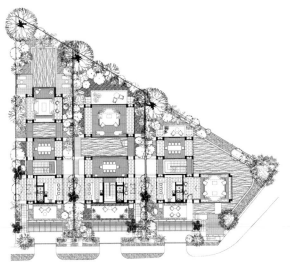

Site plan

Left A phantom outline of the Singaporean Chinese shophouse is transformed into an urbane series of town houses, floating above azure swimming pools.

Below The interiors are completely light and open, embracing the tropical gardens outside and within.

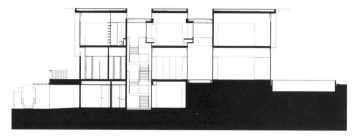

Section

House at Maple Avenue

Year of completion 2002
Location Singapore
Architect WOHA

If WOHA's design process is systemic and modular, the House at Maple Avenue both produces and counters this vocabulary. Designed for a family with four daughters, the house expresses the tension between privacy and openness in direct response to the design brief. The house is entered through a circulation corridor of thick masonry walls, which establish an introverted centre, opening into the public and private areas on either flank. Private areas face the boundary wall and open onto a series of small, enclosed courtyards; public areas are loosely defined and open onto the garden. A colonnade moves from inside to outside along the southern and western sides of the house. The planar geometry of systemic modules, sliding screens, glazing and louvres open up the spaces further, while the timber flooring continues out onto the pool deck. All effectively dissolve the formal rigours of the plan.

Yet the House at Maple Avenue is also anchored by several powerful geometries: a diagonally placed oval pool, rimmed in a raised granite ledge and surrounded by a ring of pebbles, interrupts and dominates the garden space; a spiral staircase created from a folded steel plate and sandwiched between layers of limestone hovers above a monolithic black granite base; and the master bedroom is detached from the louvre-screened building envelope, which creates a narrow double height void around the room's perimeter. The highlighting of selective elements counters the fluidity and porosity of the rest of the building, giving fixed positions from which to comprehend the house's spatial logic. It gives an added dynamism to the interior, which the architects describe as expressing the tension between feminine and masculine readings of space and form. This dynamism is extended to the flowing metal roof, which is draped over the more private areas of the house in an elegant gesture of containment. The ease with which this grand gesture is executed suggests WOHA's ability to break their own rules.

Opposite Viewed from the south west, the folded roof ends in a conventional deep eave and reveals a timber-screened box. The House at Maple Avenue is no ordinary house, but two compositional ideas fused into one: an organic roof forms a meeting with apparently roofless cubism.

Above A folded zinc roof appears to delineate the conventional line of a typical gable roof, but it does not. It is at once a wall-cladding, an insulating blanket and a piece of topography, and possibly a fragment of absent Singapore.

Section

Left The house is split along its length by its two different characters. To the left, vertical circulation is by a spiral stair, and to the right by a straight stair hung from wire rods. As with Le Corbusier's Villa Savoye, the *promenade architecturale* is made complex.

Opposite The bedrooms of the first floor hover above the ground floor formal living spaces, where the client's notable collection of Chinese porcelain and vases are on full display.

Level one

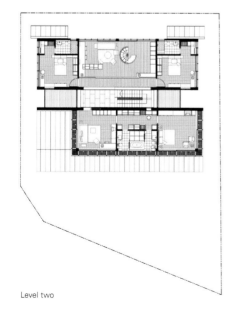

Level two

Opposite The house's split personality is seen at entry: a timber deck, a terrazzo floor, a black marble step and a folded steel-plate stair hung from the ceiling but not touching the floor. This is a study of thresholds, each more contrasting than the next.

Above An elliptical pool becomes the third major element in an intriguing hybrid of organic roof forms, a Modernist slatted box and graphic liquid landscaping.

No 1 Moulmein Rise

Year of completion 2003
Location Singapore
Architect WOHA

Left An heroic piece of new Singapore Modernism, No 1 Moulmein Rise signals a new breed of apartment tower design in Singapore: a new and powerful alternative to the standard HDB type and to the overused imported models of the West.

Opposite Seen across Singapore's treetops, No 1 Moulmein Rise appears as a realization of Le Corbusier's planned towers from La Ville Radieuse. This is a city where Modernism is not a dream, but a reality.

With the No 1 Moulmein Rise apartment complex, the familiar tube-like linearity of Singapore's urban vernacular, the Chinese shophouse, is captured in the elongated spaces of an eight-metre wide rectangular form. The building entrance opens directly onto a lap pool finished in dark green mosaic, and flanked by timber decks that descend in a series of levels along the steep incline of the site. The lobby thus acts as a verandah space, avoiding the claustrophobic entrance areas and lift wells typical of apartment blocks. The openness of this entrance, and the act of moving along a circulation corridor and upward to the residential areas, replicates the relationship of void deck to apartment level familiar to Singaporeans. The apartments are entered via private lifts that bring individual owners to the thresholds of their homes and provide them with privacy and security. The interior of each apartment, finished in soft timber and warm light colours, is divided into two zones: living and sleeping, with the services on the less scenic side of the building. Every apartment has a view of the city through a continuous façade of monsoon windows which flank the living and dining areas. These windows conceal horizontal ventilation grilles, which cleverly trap and distribute convection currents without exposing the interior spaces of the apartment to monsoonal rains. Windows open inward to aid cleaning.

The north and south façades are designed as a system of modules with the necessary depth for rain overhangs and sunshading. These modules accommodate a number of varied combinations of planter boxes, air-conditioning ledges and bay windows, which in turn are composed in a random sequence following the type of apartment behind. The service façade is a playful pattern of perforated metal panels, giving the rear of the building a slick industrial aesthetic. One rarely sees such built-in randomness in the rational grid of Singapore's apartment-scape, and its only precedent may be Tan Cheng Siong's Pearl Bank apartments (1976), where the randomness is wrapped around a pure cylindrical form. No 1 Moulmein Rise though, has a staggered profile that follows and expresses the variations in the plan and apartment configuration, as well as the gradation of the site. The narrow porous footprint, emphasis on cross ventilation and the willingness to engage with the outside environment is extremely rare in Singapore condominium design, where most developers provide introverted air conditioned environments. Here one sees WOHA's refusal to submit to such practices, welcoming the prerogatives of context: even in a multi-storey apartment complex.

Right Looking like the intricate workings of a micro computer chip, the rear of the apartment tower is modulated, like a high-rise piece of graphic design: a diagram of living units. Instead of serial repetition or mock historicism, WOHA introduce pattern and abstract formal play as a way of distinguishing this tower.

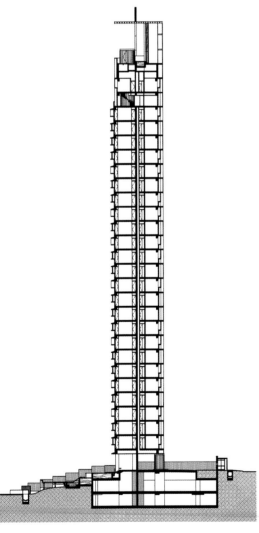

Section

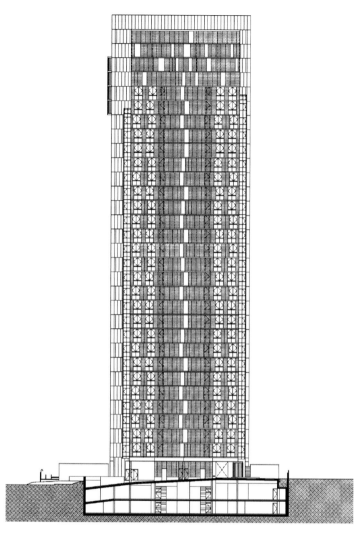

North elevation

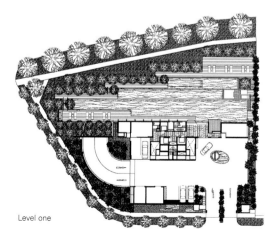

Level one

Above The soaring profile of the apartment tower is accentuated by its narrow linear slab plan, and by its crown of a cantilevering pergola, a giant fin/blade and a semi-circular glazed bay.

House at Hua Guan Avenue

Year of completion 2002
Location Singapore
Architect WOHA

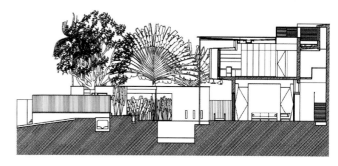

Section

Designed against one flank of its triangular site, the House at Hua Guan Avenue is a semi-detached house conceptualized as a verandah, a one sided typology opening to the view. Inspired by the client's collection of contemporary Chinese scroll paintings with their bold strokes, striking compositions and use of layering to create pictorial depth, WOHA have exaggerated the depth of a shallow site using a series of layers. The house is entered via a double height gallery, which occupies the gap between its rectangular mass and the boundary wall that contains stairs and services. This zone, typically dark and narrow in the semi-detached typology, is flooded with light and transformed into a gallery space. The living spaces lead off from this gallery, opening onto a verandah. The view through this space is to a pool running the length of the site with a small pavilion at the far corner. On the upper floor the bedrooms have cantilevered window pods that hover above the pool and can be closed off by timber screens. When open, these pods become balconies overlooking the pool below. This house captures the ambience of a tropical resort, but it does so by transforming its most public feature into a private territory. This design strategy of splicing the program gives the project a temporality that embraces the apparent vulnerability to the elements. The house thus acts like a giant verandah: it brings both the tropical light and the monsoonal rain into greater proximity, and in effect heightens its phenomenal relation to place.

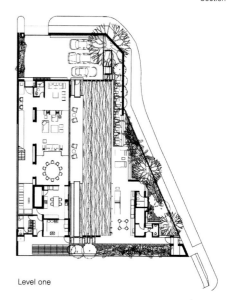

Level one

Left The northern façade of the house becomes meditation on the double-height verandah. The lap pool acts a reflective terrace, cooling and expanding the limits of the constricted site.

Above The double-height circulation gallery leads from the light-filled western entry, separating the linear body of the house from the rear party wall.

Right Looking from a living room to the pool: huge sliding glass windows can open the room entirely, creating a resort-like ambience within a constricted suburban site.

Odeon Towers Extension and MOD Living Showroom

Year of completion 2003
Location Singapore
Architect WOHA

Left The Mod Showroom floor, complete with a gallery-like collection of furniture, receives its architectural complement from above, with a ceiling of apparently weightless protruding cylinders. They are, in fact, huge planting tubs for the trees on the roof terrace.

This extension and addition to an office building in the heart of Singapore dispels any notion that WOHA is a sober architectural practice. The building comprises several elements including a furniture showroom and entrance plaza. It is both playful and urbane with various elements wedged between the sheer faces of two adjacent commercial buildings. The entry, with its narrow canyon-like verticality, is landscaped with shallow pebble-filled pools and timber decking whose colours and textures, in different shades of black and grey, emphasise their natural origins. This language of precarious surfaces that seemingly defies gravity, is wrapped and folded to form an interior space with the design of MOD Living's showroom. The expansive loft-like space of the showroom is a direct contrast to the narrow entry: huge cylindrical forms are suspended from the ceiling, encircled by slender skylights. Articulated in black and white, the showroom's minimalist geometry has the sense of being introverted: what should be a void for a circular skylight shaft is actually solid. Against this backdrop, the bright colours and amorphous shapes of designer furniture seem suspended as objects in a neutral field. Upstairs on the roof terrace, one discovers that the solid cylindrical forms are in fact massive tree planters, laid out across a timber roof deck. On one side of the building a massive lurid neon wall gives the project a dynamism: boldly shouting out its secret location to the rest of the city. The Odeon Tower Extension clearly demonstrates WOHA's willingness to engage directly with the complex urban fabric of a landscarce city, where every square meter of space is precious. On such a constricted site, WOHA's agenda is clear: place making, urbanity and spatial innovation.

Right The regularity of the column grid and descending ceiling cylinders form a perfect setting for the free arrangement of designer furniture.

Opposite The north eastern boundary wall of the complex forms a huge three dimensional billboard, which overlooks the roof terrace above the glazed box of the Mod Showroom.

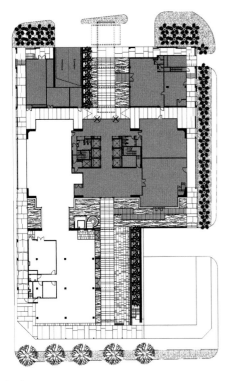

Level one

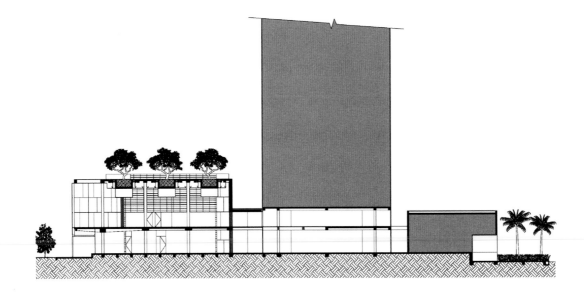

Showroom section

Church of St Mary of the Angels

Year of completion 2003
Location Bukit Batok, Singapore
Architect WOHA

Short section

Left The onyx-clad tower of the side chapel is the jewel of the complex, its form and structure revealing the shape of the cross: the translucent stone hung as if it possesses a life of light.

Opposite The internal structure of the side chapel is a cruciform reinforced concrete frame, with its blades sliced to appear as wings.

WOHA's design for St Mary of the Angels, a Franciscan parish community, comprised an extensive master plan and the design of diverse functional spaces. The Vatican II reforms of 1965, which recommended the 'in the round' spatial configuration of early Christian churches, were central to the project's brief. WOHA chose the monastic typology of a piazza flanked by breezeways, and used this central space to organize the formal elements of church, chapel, columbarium and friary. Across the complex they explored a range of forms: extroverted, introverted, singular and multiple. Each form responds to and reinforces the core values and social relationships of the religious order.

Inspired by the conceptual re-thinking of congregational space, WOHA designed the main church-space as a large atrium, suggesting an open-air urban setting most appropriate to the mission of St Francis and the communal model for churches. Departing from the cruciform plan they organized the congregation around the altar, which stands as an object on the floor of the church. Vertical structures housing private pews flank the horizontal sweep of the resulting space, resembling building blocks around a piazza.

The white Russian Oakwood seating curves slightly to receive the human form, and a large figure of Christ (designed by Teguh Osten-rik) is suspended above the altar, its image reflected in the waters of the baptismal font. The form of the cross is integrated into the ceiling in two intersecting channels of light. A slender, introverted and mysterious side chapel is flooded with yellow light filtered through Chinese Onyx panels. Its jewel-like form is the antithesis of the main church's hall-like interior.

An underground columbarium takes advantage of the natural slope in the site and is buried beneath a landscaped garden. The columbarium walls are made up of separate chambers for the interment of ashes, so that each vault is transformed into a building block in the complex.

The friary is designed as an extension to an existing structure composed of several rectangular buildings. It has been transformed into a complex of discrete blocks linked by walkways and interspersed with courtyards and pools. The remaining buildings are designed in closely grouped forms, contrasting with the openness of the church and piazza. Exercising the full scope of their design talent, WOHA have used a range of formal typologies to cater for many moods, from the most personal and contemplative to the collective experience of urban space.

Opposite The parishioners sit in solid timber pews with curved backs. The signature lamps are standard bearers amongst the crowd, each holding aloft a crucifix of lights illuminating square reflectors. Seen across the volume of the church, they appear as solid 'stars'.

Right A sculpted Christ, designed by Teguh Osten-rik, hovers beneath a crucifix of light.

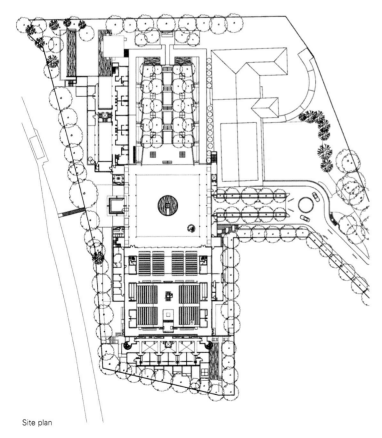

Site plan

Right The main volume of the church opens out to a cloistered court. The huge embracing roof is powerful: awesome in many respects. From this vantage point, there is also an echo of past iconic forms of Singapore Modernism, notably the NTUC Conference Hall of 1965.

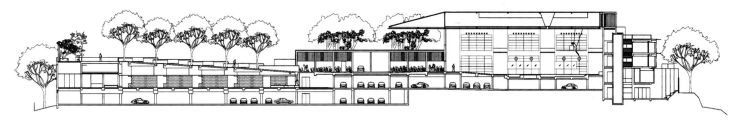

Long section

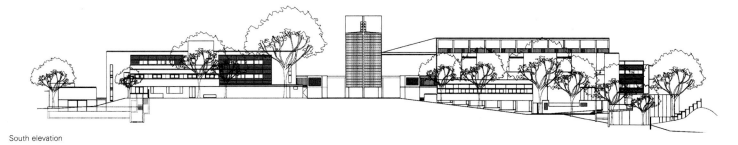

South elevation

Left The huge overhang of the main church is the equivalent of a massive 'west window': a vast umbrella with a disc of water at the cloister's centre.

Opposite The massive subterranean spaces of the columbarium are formal in character: axial and compartmented, but suffused with light from above.

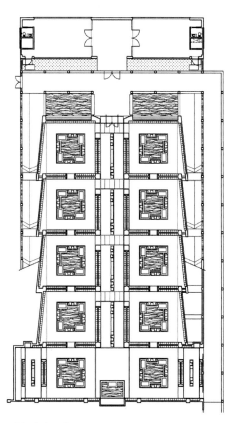

Columbarium plan